"A very readable, theologically sensitive treatment of crucial philosophical issues of central concern to the Christian faith. Dr. Naugle has done a first-rate job of covering a wide range of issues in a responsible way, while keeping the level of discourse at a truly introductory level. This book fills a needed gap in the literature, and I am delighted to endorse it."

**J. P. Moreland,** Distinguished Professor of Philosophy, Biola University; author, *Love Your God with All Your Mind*

"This fine book not only makes important explorations in Christian philosophy accessible to those who may be starting out on their intellectual journey; it also offers insights to those of us who are well along in that pilgrimage. Dr. Naugle combines solid scholarship with a firm grasp of how a biblical worldview can help to reclaim a strong Christian intellectual tradition in these confusing—but exciting—times."

**Richard J. Mouw,** President and Professor of Christian Philosophy, Fuller Theological Seminary

"Adolescent Christians entering adulthood often have plenty of zeal for the faith but stand in need of theological facility and in even greater need of philosophical awareness. This little book opens both. It inspires and summons to a life of loving wisdom (philosophy) and loving God."

**Esther Lightcap Meek,** Associate Professor of Philosophy, Geneva College; Adjunct Professor of Apologetics, Redeemer Seminary; author, *Longing to Know* and *Loving to Know*

"Although I disagree with my esteemed colleague at some points (philosophers are always arguing with each other!), this astute primer serves as a learned, well-written, deeply historical, and biblical treatment of what it means to philosophize as a follower of Jesus Christ. Readers will be richly rewarded by Professor Naugle's insights, passion, and Christian commitment to philosophy as a divine calling."

**Douglas Groothuis,** Professor of Philosophy, Denver Seminary

"David Naugle's book is an insightful guide for all 'lovers of wisdom.' It is readily understandable to the philosophical novice while at the same time offering a rich, theologically informed overview of philosophy's themes to benefit and challenge the scholar. Dr. Naugle is a philosopher who knows well the importance of worldview formation but also has a passion for thoughtful believers to be transformed into the image of Christ."

**Paul Copan,** Pledger Family Chair of Philosophy and Ethics, Palm Beach Atlantic University; author, *Loving Wisdom: Christian Philosophy of Religion*

## ~SERIES ENDORSEMENTS~

"Reclaiming the Christian Intellectual Tradition promises to be a very important series of guides—aimed at students—intended both to recover and instruct regarding the Christian intellectual tradition."

**Robert B. Sloan,** President, Houston Baptist University

"Reclaiming the Christian Intellectual Tradition is an exciting series that will freshly introduce readers to the riches of historic Christian thought and practice. As the modern secular academy struggles to reclaim a semblance of purpose, this series demonstrates why a deeply rooted Christian worldview offers an intellectual coherence so badly needed in our fragmented culture. Assembling a formidable cohort of respected evangelical scholars, the series promises to supply must-read orientations to the disciplines for the next generation of Christian students."

**Thomas Kidd,** Department of History, Baylor University

"This new series is exactly what Christian higher education needs to shore up its intellectual foundations for the challenges of the coming decades. Whether students are studying in professedly Christian institutions or in more traditionally secular settings, these volumes will provide a firm basis from which to withstand the dismissive attitude toward biblical thinking that seems so pervasive in the academy today. These titles will make their way onto the required reading lists for Christian colleges and universities seeking to ensure a firm biblical perspective for students, regardless of discipline. Similarly, campus pastors on secular campuses will find this series to be an invaluable bibliography for guiding students who are struggling with coalescing their emerging intellectual curiosity with their developing faith."

**Carl E. Zylstra,** President, Dordt College

# PHILOSOPHY

**+**

RECLAIMING THE
CHRISTIAN INTELLECTUAL TRADITION

David S. Dockery, series editor

## CONSULTING EDITORS

Hunter Baker
Timothy George
Niel Nielson
Philip G. Ryken
Michael J. Wilkins
John D. Woodbridge

## RCIT VOLUMES

*The Great Tradition of Christian Thinking*, David S. Dockery and Timothy
    George
*The Liberal Arts*, Gene C. Fant Jr.
*Political Thought*, Hunter Baker
*Literature*, Louis Markos

# PHILOSOPHY
# A STUDENT'S GUIDE

David K. Naugle

2012

**::: CROSSWAY**

WHEATON; ILLINOIS

Trade paperback ISBN: 978-1-4335-3127-9
PDF ISBN: 978-1-4335-3128-6
Mobipocket ISBN: 978-1-4335-3129-3
ePub ISBN: 978-1-4335-3130-9

---

**Library of Congress Cataloging-in-Publication Data**

Naugle, David K.
    Philosophy : a student's guide / David K. Naugle.
        p. cm.— (Reclaiming the Christian intellectual tradition)
    Includes bibliographical references and index.
    ISBN 978-1-4335-3127-9 (tp)
    1. Christian philosophy. I. Title.
BR100.N285      2012
190—dc23                                                    2012011312

---

Crossway is a publishing ministry of Good News Publishers.

| VP | | 21 | 20 | 19 | 18 | 17 | 16 | 15 | 14 | 13 | 12 |
|----|----|----|----|----|----|----|----|----|----|----|----|
| 15 | 14 | 13 | 12 | 11 | 10 | 9 | 8 | 7 | 6 | 5 | 4 | 3 | 2 | 1 |

To

Joylynn Blake, Mark Boone, Joe Brewer,
Jason Farrar, Russ Hemati, Bethany Merchant,
David Sehat, Thomas Spooner, Ryan Swindle,
Sara Mitchell, Christi Williams, Kyle Worley, and
many other philosophy majors—past, present,
future—at Dallas Baptist University

# CONTENTS

Philosophy, without his heavenly guide,
May blow up self-conceit, and nourish pride;
But, while his province is the reasoning part,
Has still a veil of midnight on his heart:
'Tis truth divine, exhibited on earth,
Gives Charity her being and her birth.

—William Cowper, "Charity"

In all these schemes [scholastic, pseudo-Lutheran, enthusiastic] the
cause of Christ becomes a partial and provincial matter within the limits
of reality. . . . [However] there are not two realities, but only one reality, and that is the reality of God, which has become manifest in Christ
in the reality of the world. . . . There are, therefore, not two spheres,
but only the one sphere of the realization of Christ, in which the reality of God and the reality of the world are united. Thus the theme
of the two spheres, which has repeatedly become the dominant fac-
tor in the history of the church, is foreign to the New Testament.

—Dietrich Bonhoeffer, *Ethics*

We destroy arguments and every lofty opinion raised against the
knowledge of God, and take every thought captive to obey Christ.

—Apostle Paul, 2 Corinthians 10:5

# SERIES PREFACE

## RECLAIMING THE CHRISTIAN INTELLECTUAL TRADITION

The Reclaiming the Christian Intellectual Tradition series is designed to provide an overview of the distinctive way the church has read the Bible, formulated doctrine, provided education, and engaged the culture. The contributors to this series all agree that personal faith and genuine Christian piety are essential for the life of Christ followers and for the church. These contributors also believe that helping others recognize the importance of serious thinking about God, Scripture, and the world needs a renewed emphasis at this time in order that the truth claims of the Christian faith can be passed along from one generation to the next. The study guides in this series will enable us to see afresh how the Christian faith shapes how we live, how we think, how we write books, how we govern society, and how we relate to one another in our churches and social structures. The richness of the Christian intellectual tradition provides guidance for the complex challenges that believers face in this world.

This series is particularly designed for Christian students and others associated with college and university campuses, including faculty, staff, trustees, and other various constituents. The contributors to the series will explore how the Bible has been interpreted in the history of the church, as well as how theology has been formulated. They will ask: How does the Christian faith influence our understanding of culture, literature, philosophy, government, beauty, art, or work? How does the Christian intellectual tradition help us understand truth? How does the Christian intellectual tradition shape our approach to education? We believe that this series is not only timely but that it meets an important need, because the secular culture in which we now find ourselves is, at best, indifferent to the Christian faith, and the Christian world—at least in its more popular forms—tends to be confused about the beliefs, heritage, and tradition associated with the Christian faith.

At the heart of this work is the challenge to prepare a generation of Christians to think Christianly, to engage the academy and the culture, and to serve church and society. We believe that both the breadth and the depth of the Christian intellectual tradition need to be reclaimed, revitalized, renewed, and revived for us to carry forward this work. These study guides will seek to provide a framework to help introduce students to the great tradition of Christian thinking, seeking to highlight its importance for understanding the world, its significance for serving both church and society, and its application for Christian thinking and learning. The series is a starting point for exploring important ideas and issues such as truth, meaning, beauty, and justice.

We trust that the series will help introduce readers to the apostles, church fathers, Reformers, philosophers, theologians, historians, and a wide variety of other significant thinkers. In addition to well-known leaders such as Clement, Origen, Augustine, Thomas Aquinas, Martin Luther, and Jonathan Edwards, readers will be pointed to William Wilberforce, G. K. Chesterton, T. S. Eliot, Dorothy Sayers, C. S. Lewis, Johann Sebastian Bach, Isaac Newton, Johannes Kepler, George Washington Carver, Elizabeth Fox-Genovese, Michael Polanyi, Henry Luke Orombi, and many others. In doing so, we hope to introduce those who throughout history have demonstrated that it is indeed possible to be serious about the life of the mind while simultaneously being deeply committed Christians. These efforts to strengthen serious Christian thinking and scholarship will not be limited to the study of theology, scriptural interpretation, or philosophy, even though these areas provide the framework for understanding the Christian faith for all other areas of exploration. In order for us to reclaim and advance the Christian intellectual tradition, we must have some understanding of the tradition itself. The volumes in this series will seek to explore this tradition and its application for our twenty-first-century world. Each volume contains a glossary, study questions, and a list of resources for further study, which we trust will provide helpful guidance for our readers.

I am deeply grateful to the series editorial committee: Timothy George, John Woodbridge, Michael Wilkins, Niel Nielson, Philip Ryken, and Hunter Baker. Each of these colleagues joins me in thanking our various contributors for their fine work. We all express our appreciation to Justin Taylor, Jill Carter, Allan Fisher, Lane Dennis, and the Crossway team for their enthusiastic support for the project. We offer the project with the hope that students will be helped, faculty and Christian leaders will be encouraged, institutions will be strengthened, churches will be built up, and, ultimately, that God will be glorified.

*Soli Deo Gloria*
David S. Dockery
Series Editor

# AUTHOR'S PREFACE

Do not be children in your thinking. Be infants in
evil, but in your thinking be mature.

—1 Corinthians 14:20

An older colleague once asked me as a novice philosopher to whom
I had hitched my philosophical wagon. At the time, I didn't know
what to say. I had learned from many, but I didn't follow anyone in
particular. Now I would say Augustine.

This guide to philosophy, written to help readers reclaim a
Christian intellectual tradition in philosophy, is Augustinian in
character. Among many possible things, this means I place faith
in the lead position before reason, and I define Christian philosophy as faith seeking understanding (*fides quaerens intellectum*).
To elaborate on this Augustinian tradition just a bit, I would say
two things. The first is that unless you believe, you will not understand. This means that in an Augustinian order of knowing (*ordo
scienta*), belief renovates reason, grace restores nature, and faith
renews philosophy. Second, Christian philosophy is essentially
Christian faith seeking *philosophical* understanding, specifically
in areas such as metaphysics, anthropology, epistemology, ethics, and aesthetics. To put it otherwise, Christian philosophy is a
reflection *of* and a reflection *on* the essential themes of canonical
Trinitarian theism (or a biblical worldview).[1] As Christian philosophers Ronda Chervin and Eugene Kevane have stated, "Christian
Philosophy is philosophizing that proceeds within a [Christian]
religious faith."[2] In this Augustinian fashion, then, I try to accom-
plish the following things in this volume.

---

[1] I owe this thought to Benno van den Toren.
[2] Ronda Chervin and Eugene Kevane, *Love of Wisdom: An Introduction to Christian Philosophy*
(San Francisco: Ignatius Press, 1988), 49.

First, I seek to highlight the importance of prolegomena for philosophy. A prolegomena, of course, is the statement of presuppositions and principles that serve as a prelude to and govern any inquiry. I want to emphasize how important it is for philosophers to state up front where they are coming from so that those who seek to learn from them will know what to expect in advance. This involves two steps. First, "know thyself," as the old oracle would have it, especially in terms of what you believe and are philosophically. Then "show thyself" prolegomenously, as a newer oracle would demand. It will take a little courage. Honesty and integrity are at stake. A prolegomena, we might say, resembles a trailer to a film or an overture to an opera. It's the general, governing word spoken beforehand and is the subject of the first chapter of this book.

Second, I desire to spell out the relationships of a Christian or biblical worldview (I'll be calling it "canonical Trinitarian theism"), Christian philosophy, and regular philosophy.[3] Sorting these out is not an easy task. I can, however, say that the movement between biblical faith and regular philosophy is a two-way street. Christianity and a Christian philosophy have a lot to offer regular philosophy. At the same time, regular philosophy contributes significantly to a Christian Weltanschauung and in shaping a Christian philosophy and philosophy (these last three domains can be difficult to distinguish). Regular philosophy, in other words, serves as a *handmaiden* to these disciplines. Yet sometimes it's the reverse. In any case, philosophy needs Christianity and vice versa. I will also address this concern in chapter 1.

Third, I will attempt to articulate elements of a Christian philosophy based on faith in God and a biblical worldview (viz.,

---

[3] Albert M. Wolters sees three levels to theorizing: (1) a worldview; (2) a philosophic understanding of things formulated out of the worldview; (3) scholarly theorizing in a particular discipline (theology and philosophy included) under the influence of a particular philosophic understanding derived from the foundational worldview. See his *Creation Regained: Biblical Basics for a Reformational Worldview*, 2nd ed. (Grand Rapids, MI: Eerdmans, 2005), 116.

canonical Trinitarian theism) in the basic philosophic subdisciplines of metaphysics, anthropology, epistemology, ethics, and aesthetics. In other words, I will try to convey something of what the Scriptures contribute to grasping reality, humanity, knowledge, morality, and beauty. This content will be covered in chapters 2 through 6.

Fourth, not only will I offer a Christian perspective on each of these main philosophical areas, but also I will try to show how a Christian philosophy in each of these subdisciplines can serve as a guide by which to interact with regular philosophy in affirmative, critical, corrective, complementary, and creative ways. At the same time, we will also investigate how regular philosophy, as handmaiden, helps to illuminate, clarify, and contribute in significant ways to understanding and applying Christian philosophy. Additionally, each main chapter in this volume will conclude with an example of one or more of these strategies in the given field.

Fifth, I intend to explain how the content of a biblical worldview shapes an understanding of the Christian philosophic vocation. I will try to show how Christian faith and philosophy frame or, perhaps, reframe the character, work, and purposes of Christian philosophers whether as professors or students. What does a gospel-shaped philosophic vocation look like? A focus will be on philosophers as lovers—of wisdom, of God as the true wisdom, and of others. This topic will engage our attention in the last chapter, one of the most important in the book.

Here are a couple of final thoughts. First, this book will not be a general survey of the various introductory issues in the different fields of philosophic study. Since there are many helpful volumes, both in Christian and non-Christian dress, that cover this ground admirably, I see no need to repeat such readily available material. Rather, my goal is to set forth a Christian philosophy in light of a particular prolegomena in several main areas of philosophic investigation.

Second, I was not able to cover every Christian topic that needed to be covered in any given area, even in overwriting the first draft of this volume considerably. The book, as you now have it, is quite abridged. Nevertheless, what the reader will find here are a few provocative ideas that will stimulate further reflection and practice for those who are called by God to wrestle with philosophy as believers. My ultimate hope is that this effort will enable Christian philosophers as *Christian* philosophers to be other-*wise*.[4]

David Naugle, ThD, PhD
Distinguished University Professor
Professor of Philosophy
Dallas Baptist University
Fourteenth Week after Pentecost 2011

---

[4] Inspired by James H. Olthius, ed., *Knowing Other-Wise: Philosophy at the Threshold of Spirituality*, 2nd ed., Perspectives in Continental Philosophy (New York: Fordham University Press, 2000).

# ✚ 1

# PROLEGOMENA

[Saint Paul] asserts that Christ is the wisdom of God and that
only Christians can attain true wisdom (1 Cor. 1–2).

—E. P. Sanders, *Paul and Palestinian Judaism*[1]

Jesus Christ is Lord of philosophy. To be sure, no one can say Jesus
is Lord, except by the Holy Spirit (1 Cor. 12:3). Certainly no one
can say Jesus is Lord *of philosophy*, and mean it, except by the
same Holy Spirit. A substantial change in inner being and outlook
fostered by Pentecostal power is surely necessary to affirm Christ's
lordship in general and his lordship over philosophy in particular.
To affirm Christ's lordship over life and philosophy, in other words,
is a function of regeneration. You must be born again (John 3).

Affirming that Jesus is Lord of philosophy is a *radically* countercultural position. It is sure to appear ludicrous to many. C. S.
Lewis (1898–1963) once bemoaned but later applauded Jesus
Christ as the "transcendental Interferer" in life.[2] Jesus is the "transcendental interferer" in philosophy as well, a proverbial "game-
changer." More theologically, Jesus Christ as incarnate Savior and
Lord interferes with philosophy by redeeming, converting, and
transforming it. He decisively shifts the philosophic paradigm.[3]

If we have a christological disposition, we should ply our
philosophic trade *coram Deo*—before the face of God. Augustine

---

[1] E. P. Sanders, *Paul and Palestinian Judaism: A Comparison of Patterns of Religion* (Minneapolis: Fortress, 1977), 505.
[2] C. S. Lewis, *Surprised by Joy: The Shape of My Early Life*, A Harcourt Brace Modern Classic (New York: Harcourt, 1955), 166.
[3] For Mark A. Noll (*Jesus Christ and the Life of the Mind* [Grand Rapids, MI: Eerdmans, 2011]), Christ and christology are the basis for the life of the Christian mind. Shouldn't he be for phi-losophy as well?

(354–430) is an example. By God's grace, he and those who have followed after him have recognized the supremacy of Jesus as the creator and redeemer of all things and knew he was the one "in whom are hidden all the treasures of wisdom and knowledge" (Col. 2:3).

Abraham Kuyper (1837–1920) certainly wanted to honor Jesus and his lordship over all creation, including education and the academic disciplines, philosophy among them. The noted Dutch polymath offered his signature proposition on the matter in these often quoted words from his inaugural address at the founding of the Free University of Amsterdam in 1880: "There is not a square inch," Kuyper thundered, "in the whole domain of our human existence over which Christ, who is Sovereign over *all*, does not cry: 'Mine!'"[4]

Kuyper's Spirit-inspired affirmation of Christ's lordship over everything is certainly a biblical notion. It is derived from God's native supremacy and sovereignty (see Ex. 9:29; Deut. 10:14; Job 41:11; Pss. 24:1; 50:12; 103:19; Dan. 4:17; cf. 1 Cor. 10:26). God's rule is especially manifest in the redemptive triumph of Jesus over sin, death, and Satan and other wicked forces that had deformed humanity and creation. In Christ, the kingdom of God was at hand (Mark 1:15). Jesus is *Christus Victor* (Col. 2:15).[5] In light of his conquest, God exalted Jesus by granting him authority and lordship over all things as the Great Commission and Paul's words make clear (Matt. 28:18; Phil. 2:9–11).

God's existence and sovereignty and Christ's lordship couldn't be more influential for the study of philosophy. Or complicating! In light of these realities, we have to ask different questions and participate in new conversations, if we are to reclaim a Christian intellectual tradition in philosophy (actually, the questions and conversations are rehabilitations of older ones). In short, we want to know how to philosophize in light of God and the gospel. We

[4] Abraham Kuyper, "Sphere Sovereignty," in *Abraham Kuyper: A Centennial Reader*, ed. James D. Bratt (Grand Rapids, MI: Eerdmans, 1998), 488.
[5] Gustav Aulén, *Christus Victor: An Historical Study of the Three Main Types of the Idea of Atonement*, trans. A. G. Hebert (Eugene, OR: Wipf & Stock, 2003).

want to grasp the philosophic implications of the Scriptures as divine revelation. Perhaps the recent turn or *re*turn to religion in philosophy and cultural affairs will facilitate discussion of these questions. That is, unless ABC prevails.[6]

Regardless, we must ask: What are Christian implications on metaphysics, anthropology, epistemology, ethics, and aesthetics? These matters constitute a veritable Gordian knot that is difficult to untie, almost as challenging as apprehending the mystery of the Trinity. Hence, we need a *prolegomena* to help us sort this out.

## PROLEGOMENA AND ITS IMPORTANCE

*Prolegomena* is derived from the neuter present passive participial form of the Greek verb *prolegein*, which means "to speak before-hand or predict." A prolegomena, or a word spoken beforehand, is a preliminary exercise to any subject matter or discussion. Its purpose is to spell out the fundamental assumptions, methods, principles, and relationships that guide any specific inquiry, especially academic ones.

Normally, theologians offer a prolegomena at the outset of their theologies to inform people of the basic concepts that are driving their reflections. From time to time, theologians' prolegomenas are quite biblical. Other times, they deploy extrabiblical ideas as the bases on which they theologize. Regardless, a theological prolegomena is quite influential. "Show me your prolegomena," says one theologian, "and I will predict the rest of your theology."[7]

A prolegomena is also philosophically prophetic. Very often, however, and this is *a very important point*, philosophers philosophize *un*prolegomenously.[8] That is, philosophy's main practitioners, Christian philosophers included, pursue the subject without giving

---

[6] ABC stands for "anything but Christianity."

[7] Gordon J. Spykman, *Reformational Theology: A New Paradigm for Doing Dogmatics* (Grand Rapids, MI: Eerdmans, 1992), 40.

[8] Immanuel Kant's *Prolegomena to Any Future Metaphysic That Will Be Able to Present Itself as a Science* (1783) is an exception.

much, if any, attention to prefatory concerns. With a tip of the hat to a presumed objectivity, many jump right into the philosophic process and churn out theories willy-nilly. We think our thoughts and theories can explain reality unmediated. We think that reality is automatically present to mind and directly expressible.

This approach, however, is naive. Philosophies have antecedents (as well as consequences), and philosophers ought to state their assumptions up front so that people will know from where they are coming. As C. S. Lewis reminds us, "For what you see and hear depends a good deal on where you are standing: it also depends on what sort of person you are."[9] Show me your prolegomena, and I can predict the rest of your *philosophy*.

## PROBLEMATIZING CHRISTIAN PROLEGOMENA

Before I build, however, I must do a little blasting. My concern is that a fair number of Christian philosophers have often relied on non-Christian sources to guide them in their thinking. Plato and the neo-Platonists, Aristotle and the Aristotelians, Descartes and the Cartesians, Kant and the Kantians, Hegel and the Hegelians, Reid and Common Sense Realists, Heidegger and the Heideggerians, and so on, have supplied various and sundry Christian philosophers with their basic principles by which they have offered an alleged Christian philosophy.

However, we must ask whether such appropriations help or hinder a Christian philosophical apprehension of God, life, and the world. For example, did aspects of neo-Platonic philosophy assumed by the early church fathers help them produce a more biblically faithful understanding of things? What influenced Ignatius of Antioch (c. 35–c. 107) to write this comment in his epistle to the Romans: "I have no delight in corruptible food nor in the pleasures of this life"?[10] Is this a Christian sentiment? Just

---

[9] C. S. Lewis, *The Magician's Nephew* (New York: Collier, 1970), 125.
[10] Ignatius, *Epistle to the Romans*, in *Ante-Nicene Fathers*, vol. 1, *Apostolic Fathers, Justin Martyr, Irenaeus*, ed. Alexander Roberts and James Donaldson (Peabody, MA: Hendrickson, 1994), 76.

how orthodox were these early Christian theologians and philosophers? Note Friedrich Nietzsche's charge that Christianity overall was basically "Platonism for the people."[11] Where does such thinking come from? It seems that various Greek conceptions damaged Christian philosophy and theology early on and in a residual way. Aren't we still struggling with the fallout of Christianized versions of stoicism, asceticism, Gnosticism, and so on?

We might also ask how more recent appropriations of aspects of rationalism, empiricism, scientism, idealism, evolutionism, processism, logical positivism, linguisticism, pragmatism, existentialism, Marxism, feminism, and so on, have affected Christian thought. Have these "isms" helped or hindered our understanding of God and his ways? What about modernism? Or postmodernism? These are huge issues. Has Christian philosophy been in thralldom to a kind of philosophic captivity over the centuries? No doubt the very idea of a "Hellenization," used here to stand for interpreting Christian truth by means of foreign outlooks ("Christ of culture") has continued unabated.

Though there will always be imperfections and impurities, we conclude, nevertheless, that a Christian philosophy requires a biblically sound prolegomena, not an interloper. A prolegomena should be indigenous to the material it directs, like a *native* guide pointing out the features of his or her homeland to visitors. Let's call it a "prolegomena to the glory of God."[12]

## A PROLEGOMENA FOR CHRISTIAN PHILOSOPHY

I begin with the claim that faith is a universal component of human nature.[13] Faith is the deepest thing within us, and, as a result, it

---

[11] Friedrich Nietzsche, *Beyond Good and Evil*, trans. Helen Zimmern (New York: Modern Library, 1954), 378.

[12] Inspired by John M. Frame, *Apologetics to the Glory of God: An Introduction* (Phillipsburg, NJ: P&R, 1994).

[13] Though supplemented by the work of others, generally these reflections on faith are from Abraham Kuyper, *Principles of Sacred Theology*, trans. J. Hendrick De Vries (Grand Rapids, MI: Baker, 1980), 125–46.

guides our thinking and living. For all of us, then, and not just Christians, "faith is the assurance of things hoped for, the conviction of things not seen" (Heb. 11:1).

If we are creatures living naturally in a God-given, faith-based mode, this means at least two things. First, we cannot divide the world between believers and nonbelievers since all people have faith and everyone believes. To be sure, objects of faith differ, and we can still divide the human race between those who possess *saving faith* and those who do not. Saving faith itself, however, is best understood as a graciously redirected function of the faith-based nature we all possess.

Second, in light of this we cannot say that religious philosophers have faith and nonreligious philosophers do not. Or that the former are biased because of faith and the latter are unbiased. Or that religious philosophers are faith-based individuals dealing with subjective values, while nonreligious philosophers are scientific and are concerned with rational, objective facts.

Rather, faith as a universal structural component of human nature levels the playing field. It means that *all* philosophers are people of faith and *all* are as biased and subjective as anyone else. In a shared way, *all* philosophers see and hear certain things, and don't see and hear others, because of who they are and where they are standing. Various and sundry *controlling stories and control beliefs* quietly guide the thoughts and lives of philosophers, even if the philosophers themselves claim to bracket their prejudices when doing philosophy.[14]

Bracketing the presuppositions we posit underneath in advance and hold by faith in our hearts, however, is impossible and doesn't happen.[15] Can we even identify our assumptions? Who can strip

---

[14] On the idea of "control beliefs," see Nicholas Wolterstorff, *Reason within the Bounds of Religion*, 2nd ed. (Grand Rapids, MI: Eerdmans, 1984), 67–70. On the concept of "controlling stories," see N. T. Wright, *The New Testament and the People of God*, vol. 1 of Christian Origins and the Question of God (Minneapolis: Fortress Press, 1992), 42.

[15] Spykman, *Reformational Theology*, 147, defines a "presupposition" etymologically as *pre-sub-ponere*, or that which is posited underneath in advance."

himself of himself or herself of herself? Even if it were possible, who would want to? Hence, presuppositions are consistently at work guiding philosophic reflection in hidden and yet powerful ways, as the moon affects the tides. Philosophers with presupposed, faith-based presuppositions are not nonreligious in nature, protestations to the contrary notwithstanding. All philosophers are religious philosophers. Secularism hasn't eliminated religion, just relocated it, especially in the direction of various forms of contemporary worship.[16] Thus, as Roy Clouser has shown, this means that religious neutrality in scholarship and theory making, philosophy included, is simply a myth.[17] Thought is a function of religion.

Another main point in this prolegomena follows directly from this. The faith of Christian philosophers ought to rest upon God, and they should derive their philosophies from canonical Trinitarian theism.[18] This is a shorthand expression for the Christian faith, referring specifically to the Trinitarian God, who has made himself and all his works known in the inspired revelation of the biblical canon from Genesis to Revelation. "Canonical Trinitarian theism" is also known, more commonly, as a biblical or Christian worldview, or as a Christian "social imaginary," if you prefer.[19] Regardless of the name, Christian philosophers ought to be Christ followers, and Christian faith ought to be the primary source of Christian philosophers' philosophy in metaphysics, anthropology, epistemology, ethics, aesthetics, and other subdisciplines.

---

[16] Pete Ward, *Gods Behaving Badly: Media, Religion, and Celebrity Culture* (Waco, TX: Baylor University Press, 2011), 19.

[17] See Roy Clouser's books *Knowing with the Heart: Religious Experience and Belief in God* (Downers Grove, IL: InterVarsity, 1999); *The Myth of Religious Neutrality: An Essay on the Hidden Role of Religious Belief in Theories* (Notre Dame: University of Notre Dame Press, 1991).

[18] What I am calling "canonical Trinitarian theism" is inspired by, though different from, William J. Abraham's proposal of "canonical theism." His proposal, which is also Trinitarian, is primarily *ecclesiological* in character, whereas mine is *bibliological*. See William J. Abraham, Jason E. Vickers, and Natalie B. Van Kirk, eds., *Canonical Theism: A Proposal for Theology and the Church* (Grand Rapids, MI: Eerdmans, 2008).

[19] Charles Taylor, *Modern Social Imaginaries* (Durham, NC: Duke University Press, 2004). See also Taylor's *A Secular Age* (Cambridge, MA: Belknap Press, 2007), chap. 4.

## MORE ELEMENTS OF A CHRISTIAN PROLEGOMENA

On this fundamental foundation about faith, let me add some additional features to a Christian philosophical prolegomena. First, in light of the doctrine of creation (Genesis 1–2), there is an important distinction between God the infinite creator and his finite creation. This prevents us from identifying God with nature (naturalism) or of identifying nature with God (pantheism). Nature is nature or creation, and not God. God is God or divine, and not nature or creation. This distinction also prevents us from equating God and humans. God is God and not people; people are people and not God (Ps. 100:3). Finally, it maintains God's sovereignty over the world he created. He is incomparably great in his person, power, and presence. Acknowledging God and his authority in this reverent way, according to Scripture, is unsurprisingly the beginning (and end) of both knowledge and wisdom (Prov. 1:7; 9:10).

Despite this ontological division, heaven and earth are not strangers. God upholds all things in existence (Jer. 33:20; Col. 2:17). All reality is holy (Isa. 6:3), "shot through with the presence of God" as Alexander Schmemann (1921–1983) has said.[20] The world is not a neutral place. It is God's. Christian philosophy must reflect these profound realities based on the distinction and intimacy between God and his world.

The next basic principle of a Christian prolegomena is that *grace restores nature* (GRN). GRN is established on the inherent connections and theological unity that exists between cosmology (nature) and soteriology (grace) in the biblical story. The doctrines of creation and redemption are deeply connected. God made a very good creation. It fell into sin. Out of covenant love, God saves and renews all things in Christ. The movement in Scripture is from creation to a new creation. God is not interested in making new

---

[20] Alexander Schmemann, *For the Life of the World: Sacraments and Orthodoxy* (Crestwood, NY: St. Vladimir's Seminary Press, 1973), 16.

things since the first things he made were very good (Gen. 1:31; Rom. 8:18–25; 2 Cor. 5:17; Col. 1:20; Rev. 21:5). To use an analogy, God created a barn. It got rats, but he didn't burn down the barn to get rid of the rats. Rather, he got rid of the rats in order to get his barn back. Christianity, in other words, is about the restoration of a sin-wrecked world.[21]

The Catholic Augustine and the Protestant Herman Bavinck (1854–1921) advocated GRN.[22] So did Russian Orthodox theologian Alexander Schmemann. "Christ came," Schmemann writes, "not to *replace* 'natural' matter with some 'supernatural' or sacred matter, but to *restore* it and to fulfill it as the means of communion with God."[23] This has tremendous philosophical implications, for if grace restores nature, or salvation renews culture, and philosophy is part of culture or nature, then salvation and grace restores philosophy. In other words, Christ restores philosophy. Saving faith enables Christian philosophers to seek philosophical understanding in him.

A third feature of a Christian philosophical prolegomena is the distinction between *structure and direction* and the associated notion of *antithesis*. Structurally, the creation was very good (Gen. 1:31). Yet, sin parasitically affected everything and all of life went in the wrong direction. Though deeply entwined, sin is still distinct from creation. To equate creation and sin is Gnostic or Manichean, not Christian. Sin is ethical misdirection. It's a moral matter, not a metaphysical one.

We can make bad use of good things, according to St. Cyril of Jerusalem (c. 318–387).[24] There is nothing wrong with sex, food,

[21] Albert M. Wolters, *Creation Regained: Biblical Basics for a Reformational Worldview*, 2nd ed. (Grand Rapids, MI: Eerdmans, 2005), 12.
[22] Augustine, "On Nature and Grace," trans. Peter Holmes and Robert E. Ernest, in vol. 5 of *Nicene and Post-Nicene Fathers*, First Series, ed. Philip Schaff (Peabody, MA: Hendrickson, 1994), 125, 142. See also Augustine's *Retractions* on "On Nature and Grace," vol. 5 of *Nicene and Post-Nicene Fathers*, 116. On grace and nature in Herman Bavinck, consult Jan Veenhof, *Grace and Nature in Herman Bavinck*, trans. Albert M. Wolters (Sioux Center, IA: Dordt College Press, 2006).
[23] Alexander Schmemann, *Of Water and the Spirit* (London: SPCK, 1976), 49.
[24] St. Cyril, *The Catechetical Lectures*, trans. Edwin H. Gifford, vol. 7 of *Nicene and Post-Nicene Fathers*, ed. Philip Schaff and Henry Wace (Peabody, MA: Hendrickson, 1994), 49.

or self, he said, since God made them all. It's their misuse that's sin. The same is true of the words we speak. We can pour into them the wine of truth or error. They are the good gifts of God, but they can be used to hurt or heal—the antithetical directions (Prov. 12:18).

John Chrysostom (c. 347–407) and Augustine espoused the structure, direction, and antithesis distinctions.[25] So did C. S. Lewis. In his earlier days, Lewis disdained the customary idea of loving the sinner (structure), but hating the sin (direction). Then he realized there was one person who had been the gracious recipient of this distinction all along, namely, himself. As he confesses in *Mere Christianity*, "However much I might dislike my own cowardice or conceit or greed, I went on loving myself. There had never been the slightest difficulty about it."[26] Lewis loved and embraced himself as structurally good, so to speak, even if he didn't like his misdirected behavior on occasion.

A fourth feature of this Christian prolegomena *is common grace*. By it, God shows nonsaving favor to all by bestowing natural gifts such as rain, sunshine, and food, on all creatures, by preserving creation and restraining sin in human affairs, and by giving diverse gifts and capacities to all people who are able to make distinctive contributions to the common good.[27] As we read in Psalm 145:9, "The Lord is good to all, and his mercy is over all that he has made."

Common grace is an antidote to taking the wrong direction at the antithetical fork in the road. Even if people go astray and misuse God's good things, common grace means that these very same people, regardless of their spiritual state, do things well and make

---

[25] John Chrysostom, *Homilies on the Statues*, trans. W. R. W. Stephens, vol. 9 of *Nicene and Post-Nicene Fathers*, First Series, ed. Philip Schaff (Peabody, MA: Hendrickson, 1994), 369; Augustine, *Confessions*, Oxford World's Classics, trans. Henry Chadwick (New York: Oxford University Press, 1998), 19.

[26] C. S. Lewis, *Mere Christianity* (New York: Macmillan, 1958), 90.

[27] Richard Mouw, *He Shines in All That's Fair: Culture and Common Grace* (Grand Rapids, MI: Eerdmans, 2001), 9.

remarkable contributions to life and the world. Beethoven and the Beatles, for example, have produced some really good music. Plato and Aristotle wrote some fine philosophy.

On the basis of common grace among philosophers, Puritan divine Cotton Mather (1663–1728) encouraged his associates to "find a friend in Plato, a friend in Socrates and . . . in Aristotle."[28] Maybe Mather got his thoughts from John Calvin (1509–1564), who espoused the same perspective.[29] So did Augustine, who came before both of them. On the basis of the Exodus story in which the Israelites plundered the gold, silver, and clothing of the Egyptians, Augustine said that believers ought to seize what is intellectually valuable from non-Christians and put it to better use in service to God.[30] Who knows, then, what insights Christian philosophers may obtain from their non-Christian colleagues? However, we must be careful not to turn our Egyptian "gold" into an idol halfway to Canaan, as Mark Boone has wisely warned.[31]

Fifth and finally, Christian scholarship is primarily *Hebraic* rather than *Hellenic or something else*. The point is that the Hebrew mind-set stands in notable experiential contrast in various points to the more abstract character of the Hellenic thought style. Hence we ask: Wouldn't neglecting the influential principles and patterns of a *Hebrew mind* deposited in the Bible seriously weaken a proper Christian scholarly understanding of God, the world, and ourselves?[32] Shall we think and live, primarily, with Greek or Hebrew lenses and hearts? Of course, we want to know

---

[28] Quoted in Leland Ryken, *Worldly Saints: The Puritans as They Really Were* (Grand Rapids, MI: Zondervan, 1986), 169.

[29] John Calvin, *Institutes of the Christian Religion*, ed. John T. McNeill, trans. Ford Lewis Battles, vol. 22 of The Library of Christian Classics, ed. John Baillie, John T. McNeill, Henry P. Van Dusen (Philadelphia: Westminster, 1960), 2.2.15.

[30] Augustine, *Teaching Christianity: De Doctrina Christiana*, vol. 11 of The Works of St. Augustine for the 21st Century, trans. Edmund Hill (Hyde Park, NY: New City Press, 1996), 159–60. See Ex. 3:22; 11:2–3; 12:35–36.

[31] Mark J. Boone, "Don't Turn Your Egyptian Gold into an Idol Halfway to Canaan." http://berry.academia.edu/MarkBoone/Talks/39443/_Dont_Turn_Your_Egyptian_Gold_into_an_Idol_Halfway_to_Canaan_.

[32] Marvin Wilson, *Our Father Abraham: Jewish Roots of the Christian Faith* (Grand Rapids, MI: Eerdmans, 1989), 135.

the essential differences between these two outlooks and whether a combination is possible.[33]

The French polymath Blaise Pascal (1623–1662), who was of sincere Christian persuasion, would certainly appreciate the Hebrew character of Christian thought since he emphasized the distinction between the God of the Bible and the "God" of the philosophers. His distinction is clear in the "Memorial" of his conversion about which he wrote in his book *Pensées*. Here he affirmed the fiery character of the God of the Hebrews, while debunking the alternative deities of scholars and philosophers as seemingly mild or timid. "Fire," he said, "God of Abraham, God of Isaac, God of Jacob, *not* of philosophers and scholars. . . . God of Jesus Christ."[34]

Christianity is Jewish, and to some extent a Christian philosophy based upon it should be as well. Yet, most Western philosophy is derived from "Athens" rather than "Jerusalem." Yet there is a difference.[35] For example, Jewish philosopher Abraham Joshua Heschel (1907–1972) observed that the "Hebrews learned in order to *revere*," whereas the Greeks learned in order to *comprehend*, and modern people learned in order to *use*.[36] The Jewish and Hellenic differences are also on display in the figures of a worshiping Israelite and an entranced Socrates:

> When Socrates was seized by a problem, he remained immobile for an indeterminate period of time in deep thought [*Symposium* 175b]; when Holy Scripture is read aloud in the synagogue, the Orthodox Jew moves his whole body ceaselessly in deep devotion and adoration. The Greek most acutely experiences the world and existence while he stands and reflects, but the Israelite

---

[33] Adolf von Harnack in his *History of Dogma* has called attention to the historically recognized influence of Hellenism, and especially Plato's philosophy, on doctrinal development in the early church.

[34] Blaise Pascal, *Pensées and Other Writings*, The World's Classics, trans. Honor Levi (New York: Oxford University Press, 1995), 178 (emphasis added).

[35] See Thorleif Boman, *Hebrew Thought Compared with Greek*, trans. Jules L. Moreau (New York: Norton, 1970); Claude Tresmontant, *A Study of Hebrew Thought*, trans. Michael F. Gibson (New York: Desclee, 1960); Duncan Black Macdonald, *The Hebrew Philosophical Genius: A Vindication* (Princeton, NJ: Princeton University Press, 1936).

[36] Abraham Joshua Heschel, *God in Search of Man: A Philosophy of Judaism* (New York: Farrar, Straus, Giroux, 1983), 34 (emphasis added).

reaches his zenith in ceaseless movement. Rest, harmony, composure, and self-control—this is the Greek way; movement, life, deep emotion, and power—this is the Hebrew way.[37]

Reverence, comprehension, or use? Detachment or the dance of devotion? These are the options. Yours?

## SUMMARY AND CONCLUSION

Hence, we have a biblically established prolegomena for Christian philosophy if we prioritize the dispositions of the Hebrew mind over those of the Greeks, if we retain the idea of common grace, if we recall that grace restores nature, if we recognize the difference between the good creational structure and its possible antithetical directions, if we remember the ontological distinction between the creator and the creation, if we base Christian philosophy on canonical Trinitarian theism, and if we remember that faith is a universal structural component of human nature. In any case, Christian philosophy is theological in character, "under the constant restraint of the Biblical presentation of the faith."[38] Christian philosophers will need pluck to be countercultural. This prolegomena often stands in critical, corrective, and creative contrast to today's approaches.

[37] Boman, *Hebrew Thought Compared with Greek*, 205.
[38] G. E. Wright, *God Who Acts: Biblical Theology as Recital* (New York: SCM Press, 1952), 109.

# ✚ 2

# METAPHYSICS

O God, Framer of the universe. . . . God who, out of nothing, has created this world. . . . God the Father of truth, the Father of wisdom, Father of true and crowning life, the Father of blessedness, the Father of that which is good and fair, the Father of intelligible light, the Father of our awakening and illumination, the Father of the pledge by which we are admonished to return to Thee.

—St. Augustine, *Soliloquies* 1.2[1]

Philosophers ask questions and think about things that most people take for granted—things such as reality or metaphysics. What is real? What is the nature of being? In this chapter, we want to understand how insights from canonical Trinitarian theism will help us shape a Christian metaphysics. We will treat the nature of humankind separately in the next chapter on philosophical anthropology.

Alfred N. Whitehead (1861–1947) may have been right when he said that Christianity "has always been a religion seeking a metaphysic."[2] Assuming certain definitions, theologian Karl Barth (1886–1968) thought that it shouldn't: "There never has been a *philosophia christiana*, for if it was *philosophia* it was not *christiana*, and if it was *christiana* it was not *philosophia*."[3] Barth may have a point. The Bible is the book of the acts of God, and Christianity is primarily a way of redemption and a moral vision,

---

[1] Augustine, *Two Books of Soliloquies*, trans. Charles C. Starbuck, vol. 7 of *Nicene and Post-Nicene Fathers*, ed. Philip Schaff (Peabody, MA: Hendrickson, 1994), 537.
[2] Alfred North Whitehead, *Religion in the Making: Lowell Lectures* (New York: Macmillan, 1926), 50.
[3] Karl Barth, *Church Dogmatics*, vol. 1, 2nd ed., trans. G. W. Bromiley, ed. G. W. Bromiley and T. F. Torrance (Peabody, MA: Hendrickson, 2010), 6.

not a metaphysical system or philosophy per se. Jesus's Beatitudes from the Sermon on the Mount in Matthew 5:2–11 might serve as exhibit A. Jewish thought refuses to reduce God, the world, people, places, or things to a "diagram" in some sort of speculative way, as Abraham Heschel declared.[4]

To be sure, Scripture as a whole and Jesus in the Sermon on the Mount don't sound exceptionally metaphysical, at least not in the Greek or Western sense. On the other hand, if metaphysics is concerned with ascertaining what is ultimately real versus mere appearances—first things as they actually are and not just as we see them (especially scientifically)—then we do not have to read very far in Scripture to find that the Jewish-Christian tradition has settled views about what God, creation, and humanity are like. Thus, Christianity throws considerable metaphysical light on all these subjects. In this rough and ready sense, then, Christianity has a metaphysic—"a tremendous notion about the world."[5] It may not be Hellenic or Hegelian in character (if you catch my drift), but it has a kind of metaphysics, divinely revealed, nonetheless.

## KNOWING GOD BY HIS DEEDS AND WORDS

God has made himself known by his deeds and words in history, disclosed in the pages of Scripture. If we lacked this revelation, we would be inventing imaginative things about him, especially by trying to peer into his own nature. Of course, we would be proud of our alleged wisdom, and yet we would be quite foolish (Rom. 1:22). To obtain true knowledge of God and to avoid deception and pride, we humbly turn in faith to God's self-revelation in Scripture. As Augustine recommends, let us "hear the oracles, and submit our weak inferences to the announcements of Heaven."[6]

---

[4] Abraham Joshua Heschel, *God in Search of Man: A Philosophy of Judaism* (New York: Farrar, Straus, Giroux, 1983), 20.

[5] Whitehead, *Religion in the Making*, 50.

[6] Augustine, *On the Morals of the Catholic Church*, trans. Richard Stothert, vol. 4 of *Nicene and Post-Nicene Fathers*, First Series, ed. Philip Schaff (Peabody, MA: Hendrickson, 1994), 44.

Here we get to know God by his deeds and words and, as it turns out, in a theistic and Trinitarian way.

We do not and cannot know God face-to-face. In fact, no one has ever "seen" God, since he alone possesses immortality and dwells in unapproachable light (1 Tim. 6:16). Should anyone see him as he is, that person, in his or her enfeebled humanity, would die (Ex. 33:20).

Even if God cannot be known directly, he can be known indirectly through his deeds and words. God has shown and told us in Scripture what he is like through a recitation of his mighty, meaningful deeds and words. John Calvin, for example, was convinced that we could know God only by what he has done rather than by metaphysical investigation: "Consequently, we know the most perfect way of seeking God . . . is not for us to attempt with bold curiosity to penetrate to the investigation of his essence . . . but for us to contemplate him in his *works* whereby he renders himself near and familiar to us, and in some manner communicates himself."[7] God is the God who acts and speaks, and by his works and words, we can know him, just as we would anyone else.

Grasping the meaning of God's mighty deeds and words in history has been central to the biblical theology movement of which G. Ernest Wright (1909–1974) was a prominent leader. There are metaphysical challenges and implications associated with the tradition of biblical theology, and Wright was careful to note them:

> The being and attributes of God are nowhere systematically presented [in Scripture] but are inferences from events. Biblical man did not possess a philosophical notion of deity when he could argue in safety and "objectivity" as to whether this or that was of God. This ubiquitous modern habit of mind which reasons from axioms and principles or universals to the concrete would have been considered as faithless rebellion against

---

[7] John Calvin, *Institutes of the Christian Religion*, ed. John T. McNeill, trans. Ford Lewis Battles, vol. 22 of The Library of Christian Classics, ed. John Baillie, John T. McNeill, Henry P. Van Dusen (Philadelphia: Westminster, 1960), 1.5.9 (emphasis added).

the Lord of history who used history to reveal his will and
purpose.[8]

If God did use the medium of his deeds and words in history to
make himself known, then to reason abstractly about him could
rightly be called "faithless rebellion." This is a significant charge
and some in the Christian philosophical community may need to
think through this.

In looking, then, to God's works and words as the way to
know him, we understand from the big biblical picture that God
has acted as the creator, judge, and redeemer of the world. In his
work of creation (Genesis 1–2), we learn something of his power
and wisdom. In his work of judgment (Genesis 3–11), we grasp
aspects of his holiness and justice. In his redemptive activity in
Christ (Genesis 12—Revelation 22), we see his kindness and grace.
Based on these works, we can confidently affirm that God is
incomparably powerful and wise, holy and just, kind and gracious.
Though God revealed himself in *particular* ways in Israel and
through Jesus and his church, his words and deeds have *universal*
implications in light of the comprehensive character of the biblical
story—the grand narrative of canonical Trinitarian theism.

## THEISM

In a more traditional metaphysical vein, this biblical view of God,
based on inferences from his words and deeds in history, is called
theism. A theistic God is personal, transcendent, immanent, and
supreme—the God who is real and is there. The theistic God is
personal like us, though infinitely greater. He is above and beyond
the world in his transcendence. He is intimately involved in the
world in his immanence. In his supremacy, God is first and last,
the Alpha and Omega, the one who is and who was and who is to
come, the Almighty (Rev. 1:8).

---

[8] G. E. Wright, *God Who Acts: Biblical Theology as Recital* (New York: SCM Press, 1952), 57–58.

The idea that a theistic version of God is essential to a Christian metaphysic must be compared and contrasted with several other perspectives on deity and reality. In *deism*, God exists transcendently over the world as its clockmaker creator. However, he is no longer immanently involved in the world. Deism, in a sense, is theism minus immanence. In *naturalism*, nature is the "whole show."[9] God doesn't exist. Only the physical cosmos is there. Naturalism, in other words, is atheism. Atheism can lead quickly to nihilism and the attempt to transcend it existentially. In *absolute pantheism*, all things are ultimately one thing (monism), and that one thing is God (atheism is also a monism in positing nature alone as religiously insignificant). God is all and all is God, appearances to the contrary notwithstanding. In *polytheism*, there are many gods and many goddesses, like those worshiped by the Egyptian, Greek, Roman, and Nordic peoples (Americans, too, in their worship of sex, fame, and fortune). There are almost as many deities as there are realms of life over which they have supernormal, if not supernatural, jurisdiction, such as agriculture and war. Most of the world's great religions are polytheistic, save the great monotheisms of Judaism, Islam, and Christianity. *Panentheism* stresses the interactive relationship of God and nature. It seeks to avoid the excesses of either theistic transcendence or pantheistic immanence. God is active in the world's evolutionary process, neither separated from nor identified with the cosmos. God is to the world as a soul is to the body. Theism, therefore, is not deism, naturalism, absolute pantheism, polytheism, or panentheism. It is different because God is the supreme, personal, transcendent, immanent creator, judge, and redeemer who is there.

Theism, however, can easily slide toward a Greek metaphysical construct if we are not careful. Rather than ontologizing God as the Greeks might do, we must emphasize that the New Testament theistic God is the God who comes lovingly near in the incarnate

---

[9] C. S. Lewis, *Miracles: A Preliminary Study* (New York: Macmillan, 1947), 12.

Christ and his cross. God is a suffering servant, which, of course, no one would expect. Theism, therefore, is not only about the existence and character of God, but also about the fact that he is close to us in love.[10] The mighty deed of his mighty deeds is "that while we were still sinners, Christ died for us" (Rom. 5:8). The God of the Bible is a God with wounds.[11]

## TRINITARIANISM

The theistic God of the Bible is also Trinitarian. As to what God is in his nature, God the Trinity is one *and* three, and the three *and* one, or if you prefer, three *in* one, and one *in* three. That is, God is one, indivisible, divine substance, yet he subsists as three distinguishable co-divine, co-equal, and co-eternal persons—the Father, the Son, and the Holy Spirit. As I heard one of my professors say, there is the one divine *what* or substance and the three divine *whos* or persons. These opening lines of the Athanasian Creed capture the church's vision of God the Trinity.

> We worship one God in Trinity, and Trinity in Unity, neither confounding the Persons nor dividing the Substance. For there is one Person of the Father, another of the Son, and another of the Holy Spirit. But the Godhead of the Father, of the Son, and of the Holy Spirit is all one, the Glory equal, the Majesty coeternal. . . . So the Father is God, the Son is God, and the Holy Spirit is God. And yet there are not three Gods, but one God.

The "Shield of the Trinity" diagram helps us understand a bit more about this Trinitarian mystery. It conveys three basic ideas: (1) each of the three persons of the Trinity is fully God—the Father is fully God, the Son is fully God, and the Holy Spirit is fully God; (2) the fullness of the one God is present in each of the

---

[10] Based on Eberhard Jüngel, *God as the Mystery of the World: On the Foundation of the Theology of the Crucified One in the Dispute between Theism and Atheism*, trans. Darrell L. Guder (Grand Rapids, MI: Eerdmans, 1983).
[11] Os Guinness, *Unspeakable: Facing Up to Evil in an Age of Genocide and Terror* (San Francisco: Harper San Francisco, 2005), 145–48.

three persons of the Trinity—God is the Father, God is the Son, and God is the Holy Spirit; and (3) the three persons of the Trinity are each distinct—the Father is not the Son and the Son is not the Father, the Father is not the Holy Spirit and the Holy Spirit is not the Father, and finally, the Son is not the Holy Spirit and the Holy Spirit is not the Son. Any kind of Christian metaphysics must, therefore, be Trinitarian in character.

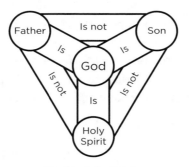

*Shield of the Trinity*

In so expressing God the Trinity, we must ask if we are departing from our commitment to knowing God on the basis of his acts and words in history. Possibly, but hopefully not. In what is called the "economic" trinity, which focuses on what God does, he is the one who stands behind all the action in the world as its fundamental mystery. We know about God and his Trinitarian nature in his works of creation, judgment, and redemption and in his words about these astonishing deeds. Perhaps, then, Trinitarianism is just a way, with logical assist, to articulate the truths about him in the big story of the Scriptures.

Vestiges of the triune God (*vestigia trinitatis in creatura*) can be detected throughout the cosmos with metaphysical and anthropological consequences. For example, Augustine believed that a Trinitarian trace is to be seen in a lover, a beloved, and their shared love. He also thought that the human mind comprised of intellect, memory, and will and that our capacity of sight consisting of an object seen, the attention of the mind, and external vision were reflections of the Trinity.[12] For Tertullian, the Trinity as one God in three persons may be detected in a plant as root, tree, and fruit; in water as a fountain, river, and stream; and in light as sun, ray, and apex.[13] Greek Orthodox theologian Georges Florovsky believed that the church herself was a Trinitarian token, "a likeness in which many become one."[14] Florovsky believed that the unity and diversity of Christian relationships in the church must be preserved for Trinitarian reasons: "The idea of the [one] organism must be supplemented by the idea of a symphony of personalities, in which the mystery of the Holy Trinity is reflected."[15] Human beings, all creation, and the church are quite possibly Trinitarian remnants.

## CREATION

This theistic, Trinitarian God is known in his works, and his works begin with *creation*. Genesis 1:1 sets forth the big idea: "In the beginning, God created the heavens and the earth." The implications of this scriptural teaching are, of course, total. They contribute in at least three ways to a Christian metaphysic. The first is that the world in which we live is, in fact, *created*, and not *nature*. The world is not just "there, and that is all," as Bertrand Russell (1872–1970) once said in a debate with Frederick Copleston (1907–1994). Instead, the world is God's creation, and we need to make this wonderful rediscovery and of the divinely bestowed wisdom that comes along with it.

The doctrine of creation is foundational to everything else. It is the place where the divine-human drama, tragedy, and comedy

---

[12] Augustine, *On the Holy Trinity*, trans. Arthur West, vol. 3 of *Nicene and Post-Nicene Fathers*, ed. Philip Schaff (Peabody, MA: Hendrickson, 1994), bks. 9–12.
[13] Tertullian, *Against Praxeas*, trans. Peter Holmes, vol. 3 of *Ante-Nicene Fathers*, ed. Alexander Roberts and James Donaldson (Peabody, MA: Hendrickson, 1994), 603.
[14] Georges Florovsky, *Bible, Church, Tradition: An Eastern Orthodox View*, in *The Collected Works of Georges Florovsky*, vol. 1 (Belmont, MA: Nordland, 1972), 44.
[15] Ibid., 67.

unfold. It is the object of human cultural development. It has been unhappily deformed by sin. God has graciously redeemed or restored creation in Christ. Thus a metaphysic of creation is deeply religious in content and character. "Christianity," as Clarence Glacken has stated, . . . is a religion and a philosophy of creation."[16]

A second biblically derived metaphysical trait of creation is *its doxological and sacramental character*. God brought the entire cosmos into existence for his glory. Familiar passages such as Psalm 19:1 and Romans 1:20 tell us, respectively, that the skies declare God's glory, and that his eternal power and divine nature are on display in the things he made. The world is God's glorious workmanship—the veritable theater of his glory—as many in various Christian traditions have noted. "Wherever you cast your eyes," wrote John Calvin, "there is no spot in the universe wherein you cannot discern at least some sparks of his glory."[17]

To say that creation is sacramental is to say that it is sacred in character, sin notwithstanding. All ground is holy ground. We best take off our sandals regardless of location. Insofar as that creation is holy, one of its primary vocations is to tell us about God and to draw us into deeper communion with him. We are moved with thanksgiving and praise—from the creation and its gifts to the Creator as giver. This is called a "eucharistic" view of life and the world. Alexander Schmemann states it like this:

> All that exists is God's gift to man, and it all exists to make God known to man, to make man's life communion with God. It is divine love made food, made life for man. God *blesses* everything He creates, and, in biblical language, this means that He makes all creation the sign and means of His presence and wisdom, love and revelation: "O taste and see that the Lord is good."[18]

---

[16] Clarence J. Glacken, *Traces on the Rhodian Shore: Nature and Culture in Western Thought from Ancient Times to the End of the Eighteenth Century* (Berkeley, CA: University of California Press, 1967), 168.

[17] Calvin, *Institutes of the Christian Religion*, 1.5.1.

[18] Alexander Schmemann, *For the Life of the World: Sacraments and Orthodoxy* (Crestwood, NY: St. Vladimir's Seminary Press, 1973), 14.

Thus, our intercourse with the world puts us in communion with God. As Schmemann states, "The world was created as the 'matter,' the material of one all-embracing eucharist, and man was created as the priest of this cosmic sacrament."[19] The familiar sacraments themselves, such as baptism and communion, are concentrated ecclesial expressions of this fundamental Christian interpretation of life.

A third Christian metaphysical trait of creation is its prudential character. All reality is pervaded with *divine wisdom*. God's creativity, design, and skillfulness are evident in his multiple works (Ps. 104:24). There is, therefore, an objective reality that God has wisely ordained, from the leaves that flutter on the trees to the galaxies. If we wish to be wise ourselves, we must apprehend that reality and order our lives accordingly. We must live with the grain of the universe, not in opposition to it, lest we get a splinter, to put the matter metaphorically. Hence, wisdom has objective and subjective sides, well defined as "ethical conformity to God's creation."[20] Otherwise, we are fools.

Proverbs 9 conveys the matter poetically. Lady Wisdom invites us to her house for a feast of God's true wisdom. If we refuse her invitation, a boisterous Lady Folly may seduce us and force us to partake of her banquet of pseudo-wisdom instead. Whether one reverentially fears the Lord is the determinative issue (Prov. 1:7; 9:10; 15:33). Of course, the consequences of the decision about which to heed and whom to fear are personally and culturally massive (Prov. 8:32–36).

## IMPLICATIONS

Insofar as the world itself is a doxological, sacramental, and prudential reality created by a theistic, Trinitarian God, the metaphysical implications are notable. First, views of reality that eliminate

---

[19] Ibid., 15.
[20] James Fleming, *Personalities of the Old Testament* (New York: Scribners, 1939), 502.

a spiritual, supernatural, or transcendent principle are unacceptable. Naturalism has resulted in the demise of metaphysics itself. Despite its prevalence in academia, it is not a Christian metaphysical option. Idealism has been considered a possible Christian position on metaphysics in specifying that creation is a function of God's thoughts.[21] Reality is rooted in the divine mind and is not dependent on human perception, as Ronald Knox (1888–1957) stated in his famous limerick:

> There was a young man who said, "God
> Must think it exceedingly odd
> If he finds that this tree
> Continues to be
> When there's no one about in the Quad."

> REPLY
> Dear Sir:
> Your astonishment's odd:
> I am always about in the Quad.
> And that's why the tree
> Will continue to be,
> Since observed by
> Yours faithfully,
> GOD.

At the same time, idealism can be rather impersonal. Perhaps, then, some version of commonsense Christian realism is best. God made a real world on the basis of a divine blueprint. He holds it in existence, rules over it providentially, restores it from sin, and will direct it to its appointed end, ultimately for doxological purposes. In trying to figure out what is metaphysically real about this world, we must remember that we are philosophizing on God's dime. We are guests investigating a cosmos

---

[21] The possible orthodoxy of George Berkeley's version of Christian idealism has been defended in James S. Spiegel, "The Theological Orthodoxy of Berkeley's Immaterialism," *Faith and Philosophy* 13 (April 1996): 216–35.

not our own. He is the maker and owns the house. We are just renters.

Second, our stewardly investigation of the world is designed to tell us something about the grandeur of its maker. As "we take upon ourselves the mystery of things as if we were God's spies,"[22] we do so with the possibility of learning more about the author of reality himself. At least we should, whether our investigation is about the origin, nature, and goals of the world itself (cosmogony, cosmology, teleology), the question of universals (realism, nominalism, conceptualism), the nature of particular things (bundle theory and substratum and substance views), the debates over freedom and necessity (determinism and free will), on the relationship of minds and bodies (dualism and monism), and so on. As Christian philosophers come to know and love these things, the more they should come to know and love the God who made them.

Third, creation-based wisdom is astonishingly broad. God's laws govern everything. All of life is doxological, sacramental, and prudential. Thus, Solomon's own wisdom was correspondingly botanic and zoological as well as explicitly moral and spiritual (1 Kings 4:29–34). Ancient Greek philosophy was analogously comprehensive. Aristotle, for example, wrote treatises not just on metaphysics and ethics, but also on the heavens, meteorology, memory, sleep, dreams, animals, plants, colors, and so on.[23] This founding philosophical father once said, "There are as many parts of philosophy as there are kinds of substance," and he added, "It is the function of the philosopher to be able to investigate all things."[24] This is a reason why science was originally called "natural philosophy" and became the seedbed of the modern sciences. A Christian metaphysics naturally possesses a comprehensive

---

[22] Shakespeare, *The Tragedy of King Lear*, in *The Oxford Shakespeare: The Complete Works*, 2nd ed., ed. John Jowett, William Montgomery, et al. (New York: Oxford University Press, 2005), 1180.
[23] See the table of contents to Aristotle, *The Complete Works: The Revised Oxford Translation*, 2 vols., Bollingen Series LXXI•2, ed. Jonathan Barnes (Princeton, NJ: Princeton University Press, 1984).
[24] Aristotle, *Metaphysics*, trans. W. D. Ross, *The Complete Works*, 2:1585–86.

character. It is possible to obtain divine insight and to live skill-fully in all realms of reality as God has ordained them, even in art and agriculture (see Ex. 31:1–5; Isa. 28:23–29).

## CONCLUSION: THE ONE AND THE MANY

In reclaiming a Christian intellectual tradition in philosophy, one of the purposes of this volume is to provide a guide for Christian philosophers by which they may interact with regular philosophy across its subdisciplines in affirmative, critical, corrective, and cre-ative ways. God's Trinitarian nature provides a resource to interact critically and creatively with, if not solve, the perpetual metaphys-ical question of "the one and the many."

The issue of the one and the many is found in the word *uni-verse* itself. What makes the universe, indeed, a *uni-verse*, that is, a world in which there is a *unity* that ties all the *diversity* together? In addressing this seminal problem, most have overemphasized either the one (monism) or the many (pluralism), with perhaps a couple of exceptions. Regardless, William James believed that the one and the many was "the most central of all philosophic problems."[25]

Is not the explanation for the singularity and plurality of real-ity to be found in the Trinitarian God? In God himself, there is a unified diversity, or a diversified unity—a threeness and a oneness, a oneness and a threeness—and the whole world of many parts (its many-ness) finds its coherence in the one God, the creator and redeemer of heaven and earth. God is thus the reference point for all reality. He is the interpretive key who provides the meaning for all things. He ties it all together in himself. Furthermore, the incar-nation of Jesus Christ as the God-Man is also a key to solving the problem of the one (God) and the many (man). Jesus re-members a fragmented, dis-membered world in himself.[26] He reconciles all

---

[25] William James, *Pragmatism: A New Name for Some Old Ways of Thinking: Popular Lectures on Philosophy* (New York: Longmans, Green, 1907), 129.

[26] C. Marvin Pate, *From Plato to Jesus: What Does Philosophy Have to Do with Theology?* (Grand Rapids, MI: Kregel, 2011), 12.

things through the blood of his cross and ties them together again (Col. 1:19–23). If physics as a naturalistic science is seeking a Grand Unified Theory (GUT), or a Theory of Everything (TOE), or a Unified Field Theory (UFT) to put it all together, it should look to a Trinitarian metaphysics for a solution. God is the author of all things and unites them together in himself. If we make this discovery, "then we would know the mind of God."[27]

---

[27] Stephen Hawking, *The Theory of Everything: The Origin and Fate of the Universe* (Beverly Hills, CA: New Millennium Press, 2002), 167.

3

# PHILOSOPHICAL ANTHROPOLOGY

Who and what man is, is no less specifically and emphatically declared by the Word of God than who and what God is. The Word of God essentially encloses a specific view of man, an anthropology, an ontology of this particular creature.

—Karl Barth

Philosophers ask questions and think about things that most people take for granted—things such as philosophical anthropology and views of humanity. What is a person? What is human nature? In this chapter, we want to see how insights from canonical Trinitarian theism help us form a Christian philosophical anthropology.

Let's resurrect the old idea that we human beings are *microcosms* of the universe and God. The concept of microcosm and macrocosm is that parts of the universe resemble other parts, and that human beings as microcosms, or little worlds, epitomize macrocosms or great worlds—either the universe as a whole or some part of it or God.[1] Though moderns might be inclined to call this idea a "poetic fancy,"[2] there is biblical grounding for it. Human beings, according to Genesis 1, are the image and likeness of God.

Aristotle was the first to use the word *microcosm*, though the idea precedes and follows him voluminously.[3] Heraclitus discussed

---

[1] George P. Conger, *Theories of Macrocosms and Microcosms in the History of Philosophy* (New York: Columbia, 1922), *xiii*.
[2] Ibid., *xviii*.
[3] See Aristotle, *Physics*, trans. W. D. Ross, vol. 1 of *The Complete Works of Aristotle: The Revised Oxford Translation*, Bollingen Series LXXI•2, ed. Jonathan Barnes (Princeton: Princeton University Press, 1984), 422.

it. It was used frequently in the Renaissance and eventually became a common literary trope, though for most writers it was more than just a figure of speech.[4] For example, in a splendid passage in *Paradise Lost,* John Milton extols human rule and rationality that show us to be a microcosm of God, whom we should acknowledge gratefully as the source of our lofty capacities and roles in creation:

> . . . A creature who not prone
> And brute as other creatures, but endued [= endowed]
> With sanctity of reason, might erect
> His stature, and upright with front serene
> Govern the rest, self-knowing, and from thence
> Magnanimous to correspond with Heaven,
> But grateful to acknowledge whence his good
> Descends; thither with heart and voice and eyes
> Directed in devotion, to adore
> And worship God supreme, who made him chief
> Of all his works.[5]

We are not just animals on four legs or, in a current idiom, primates who use cell phones! Instead, we are upright creatures who possess the ability to think and reason in self-reflective and self-conscious ways. As a result, we are able to know ourselves and rule the world as a *microcosm* of God himself. In light of our creaturely honor, we might be tempted to try to take God's place. Of course, that's impossible and will never happen. Rather, we should be gratefully devoted to God for the gifts and roles he has given us in his world.

Here is a little thought experiment: What if we weren't microcosms of God? What if we weren't his image and likeness?[6] What if there was no God in whose image we are created? Would atheism

---

[4] Taken from John Calvin, *Institutes of the Christian Religion*, ed. John T. McNeill, trans. Ford Lewis Battles, vol. 22 of The Library of Christian Classics, ed. John Baillie, John T. McNeill, Henry P. Van Dusen (Philadelphia: Westminster, 1960), 1.5.3.
[5] John Milton, *Paradise Lost*, in *The Portable Milton*, ed. Douglas Bush (New York: Penguin, 1977), 410.
[6] I owe this thought to Chad Kidd.

and such an anthropocentrism enhance our already prevalent misanthropic tendencies? Might this condition barbarize us even more?

On the other hand, what if God exists and we *are* his image and likeness? What would be the implications of theism and such a dignified human status? Would it change our views of ourselves? Would it change our attitudes, words, and behaviors toward one another? It did for C. S. Lewis. In recognizing human beings as bearers of God's image and glory, he said our neighbors are the holiest objects presented to our senses, except for the elements of the Blessed Sacrament itself.[7] The apostle James believed that a recognition of our identity as God's likeness should change the way we talk about others:

> With it [our tongue] we bless our Lord and Father, and with it we *curse people who are made in the likeness of God.* From the same mouth come blessing and cursing. My brothers, these things ought not to be so. (James 3:9–10)

The way we talk about others reveals our anthropological attitudes in general, what we really think about people and their identity. Are they evolutionary products only? Are they God's image and likeness? It makes a difference.

Our ability to use language itself affirms our uniqueness, according to Mortimer Adler. In his book *The Difference of Man and the Difference It Makes*, he argues that we human beings differ in *kind* and not just in *degree* from other creatures because we possess "the power of syntactical speech."[8] Though scientists in many fields have pointed this out, for Adler this linguistic trait is *the* human difference that makes a difference.

True enough as far as it goes, but I think we need to say more. *Why* are we distinguished users of language? *Why* do we have

---

[7] C. S. Lewis, "The Weight of Glory," in *The Weight of Glory and Other Addresses* (Grand Rapids, MI: Eerdmans, 1949), 15.
[8] Mortimer J. Adler, *The Difference of Man and the Difference It Makes* (Cleveland: Meridian, 1967), 43.

the power of syntactical speech? Does language use *itself* really explain how we are different in kind? What makes for the major differences between ourselves and other creatures?

It must be because we are a microcosm of the macrocosm, out-and-out the image and likeness of God, as the Scriptures teach (see Gen. 1:26–27; 5:1; 9:6; Pss. 8:4–8; 82:6; John 10:34; 1 Cor. 11:7; Eph. 4:24; Col. 3:10; James 3:9).

> Then God said, "Let us make man in our image, after our like-ness. And let them have dominion over the fish of the sea and over the birds of the heavens and over the livestock and over all the earth and over every creeping thing that creeps on the earth." So God created man in his own image, in the image of God he created him; male and female he created them. (Gen. 1:26–27)

We are profoundly like God. This is bound to be what enables us to use language and makes us different in kind. As one Old Testament scholar declared: "Man is the one *godlike* creature in all the created order. . . . By the doctrine of the image of God, Genesis affirms the dignity and worth of man, and elevates all men—not just kings or nobles [or movie stars and athletes]—to the highest status conceivable, short of complete divinization."[9]

Certainly, to know that we are God's image and likeness is valuable. It's another thing, however, to understand what this means exactly. How should we interpret the phrase "the image and likeness of God"? What are its philosophical implications?

## IMAGO DEI

First, to be God's image means that we are like God as total, embodied beings in substance, relationships, and function. We are not God, to be sure. But we are sufficiently like him to represent him in the world in our various roles. Our identity as God's image comes to expression as we image him in this world. On the basis of

---

[9] D. J. A. Clines, "The Image of God in Man," *Tyndale Bulletin* 19 (1968): 53 (emphasis added).

evidence gathered from the Old Testament and the ancient Near East, D. J. A. Clines summarizes the *imago Dei* in a similar way.

> Man is created not *in* God's image . . . but *as* God's image, or rather to be God's image, that is to deputize [humankind] in the created world [as agents] for the transcendent God who remains outside the world order. That man is God's image means that he is the visible corporeal representative of the invisible, bodiless God; he is representative rather than representation, since the idea of portrayal is secondary in the significance of the image. However, the term "likeness" is an assurance that man is an adequate and faithful representative of God on earth. The whole man [person] is the image of God, without distinction of body and spirit. All mankind [people], without distinction, are the image of God.[10]

This definition, combined with insights from other biblical texts about humanity, leads to the following anthropological points. The first feature of human beings is that we are primarily *lovers*. Since God is love (1 John 4:8), this must be our basic nature as well. We are the kinds of creatures who love people, places, and things. "*Homo sapiens*," "*homo faber*" . . . yes, but first of all, "*homo adorans*."[11] In other words, we think thoughts and we make things, but first and foremost, we are the kinds of creatures who adore. Life matters to us, as Martin Heidegger (1889–1976) pointed out. We care or are beings of care.[12]

We do, however, have to care about things in a proper way. There is a divinely ordained order to our loves (*ordo amoris*). According to the first great commandment, we are to love God first and foremost. According to the second great commandment, we are to love others as we love ourselves (Lev. 19:34; Deut. 6:5; Matt. 22:34–40; Luke 10:25–28). We will reap what we sow in

---

[10] Ibid., 101.
[11] Alexander Schmemann, *For the Life of the World: Sacraments and Orthodoxy* (Crestwood, NY: St. Vladimir's Seminary Press, 1973), 15.
[12] Martin Heidegger, *Being and Time*, trans. John Macquarrie and Edward Robinson (New York: Harper & Row, 1962), 242.

regard to this arrangement. If we disregard the proper order and responsibilities of love, then we violate our nature and will find ourselves in a painful state. If we submit to them, then we might discover the deep meaning of happiness.

Hence, the most important anthropological questions we can ask and answer revolve around our loves. What do we love? How do we love what we love? What do we expect to receive from the things we love? Is love a feeling or emotion? Or is it a choice of the will or an action? Might love be a combination of both emotion and action? What might constitute a biblical philosophy of caring and loving?

Second, God made us to be his image and likeness as *male and female* for relationships, especially in the context of *marriage and family*. Both women and men are God's image, and we were made to be social beings in relationships with each other especially as husband and wife along together with our offspring. Hence, we have family life.

Genesis 1:27–28 closely associates our identity as the image of God with our sexual identities and the procreative purposes:

> So God created man in his own image, in the image of God he created him; *male and female he created them*. And God blessed *them*. And God said to them, "*Be fruitful and multiply* and fill the earth and subdue it, and have dominion over the fish of the sea and over the birds of the heavens and over every living thing that moves on the earth."

The only thing about the original creation that was not good was the man's isolation and aloneness. It was bad for the first man to be by himself. God rectified his solitary state of affairs by creating the woman, giving her to the man, and establishing the institution of marriage. "Therefore," according to Genesis 2:24, "a man shall leave his father and his mother and hold fast to his wife, and they shall become one flesh." This text along with the Song of Solomon and various other biblical teachings supply the Christian thinker with considerable input for a Christian vision of manhood and womanhood, sexuality, marriage, and family.

In this light, we can ask, for example, Were Plato's marriage laws in the *Republic* wise?[13] Did he recommend infanticide, as some think?[14] Additionally, how might a Christian anthropology derived from Scripture interface with contemporary feminist philosophies of the body, philosophies of homosexuality, and the issue of same-sex marriage? Are sexual orientations and practices socially constructed or biologically driven?

We can at least say that our sociality was God's idea, even though sin has significantly corrupted this sensitive relational area of human life. As whole persons, then, we encounter God first and then each other as male or female in meaningful relationships. God inscribed a deep social purpose in our hearts. "For this is the message that you have heard from the beginning, that we should love one another" (1 John 3:11).

Third, God made us as his image and likeness *to rule over the world and to be culture makers*. In the ancient Near East, only royalty were considered to be the image of God. Kings would set up images of themselves to convey their presence and authority over newly conquered lands. Pagan worshipers also set up physical images of their absentee gods or goddesses in temples to represent their existence and rule. In a similar way, the transcendent God has set up human beings as his image and likeness to be the royal rulers of his creation. Our identity as God's image is closely associated with our dominion activities, as Genesis 1:26 suggests:

> Then God said, "Let us make man in our *image*, after our *likeness*. And let them have *dominion* . . ."

---

[13] G. M. A. Grube, "The Marriage Laws in Plato's Republic," *The Classical Quarterly* 21 (April 1927): 95–99.

[14] See Plato's *Republic* 459d-e, 460c, 461b-c.

This task of having dominion over the earth is rightly seen as a "cultural" mandate. Our culture-forming activities are manifested early on in Genesis 2 as the first man nurtures and keeps Eden-garden. Whether over land, sea, or air, fish, bird, or beast, men and women individually and together as the *imago Dei* are to develop the possibilities hidden in the womb of creation, both natural and human.[15] This would include technology—commissioned, fallen, and redeemed—as it develops from the primeval garden to the New Jerusalem.[16] Ludwig Köhler sees the dominion mandate as a cultural mandate, manifested especially in the origins of architecture and clothes making with implications for education and vocation today:

> The task given to man to rule over creation as it was in former times and as it is down to the present day: This is the commission to establish civilization. It applies to all men, and it embraces every age. There is no human activity which is not covered by it. The man who found himself with his family on a plain exposed to ice-cold wind and first laid a few stones one upon another and invented the wall, the basis of all *architecture*, was fulfilling this command. The woman who first pierced a hole in a hard thorn or fishbone and threaded a piece of animal sinew through it in order to be able to join together a few shreds of skin, and so invented the needle, sewing, the beginning of all the art of *clothing*, was also fulfilling this command. Down to the present day, all the instructing of children, every kind of school, every script, every book, all our technology, research, science and teaching, with their methods and instruments and institutions, are nothing other than the fulfillment of this command. The whole of history, all human endeavor, comes under this sign, this biblical phrase.[17]

On this ground we grasp something of the profound nature

---

[15] Albert M. Wolters, *Creation Regained: Biblical Basics for a Reformational Worldview*, 2nd ed. (Grand Rapids, MI: Eerdmans, 2005), 43.

[16] For a biblical philosophy of technology, see John Dyer, *From the Garden to the City: The Redeeming and Corrupting Power of Technology* (Grand Rapids, MI: Kregel, 2011).

[17] Ludwig Köhler, *Der hebräische Mensch*, quoted in Hans W. Wolff, *Anthropology of the Old Testament*, trans. Margaret Kohl (Philadelphia: Fortress, 1973), 164 (emphasis added).

and meaning of our tasks in the world. Philosophy is one of these tasks. If done for God, it should be done in a different, even theological, key. In any case, from this survey we see how love, relationships, and culture making are constitutive of our identity as the image and likeness of God—the visible corporeal representative of the invisible, bodiless God on the earth.

## THE INCARNATION

Jesus Christ was the full and complete image of God on the earth (see Col. 1:15). As the eternal Son of God and second person of the Trinity, the Word or *Logos* of God became flesh and dwelt among us (John 1:14). Jesus bought a house and "moved into the neighborhood," as Eugene Peterson paraphrases this text in *The Message*. His "divinity-in-humanity" or "humanity-in-divinity" is the mystery of the incarnation (1 Tim. 3:16a).

The word *incarnation* literally means "in the flesh"—God with skin on him, so to speak. Though the word *incarnation* is not found anywhere in the Bible, nevertheless it conveys the idea that in Jesus we see the perfect and permanent union of humanity and deity without either of these natures being impaired.[18] The orthodox view of the incarnation was spelled out well in these words of the Chalcedonian Creed (451):

> Therefore, following the holy fathers, we all with one accord teach men to acknowledge one and the Same Son, our Lord Jesus Christ, at once complete in Godhead and complete in manhood, truly God and truly man consisting of a reasonable soul and body; of one substance with the Father as regards his Godhead, and at the same time of one substance with us as regards his manhood; like us in all respects, apart from sin; as regards his Godhead, begotten of the Father before all ages, but yet as regards his manhood begotten, for us . . . and for our salvation, of Mary the Virgin, the God-bearer.

---

[18] *The Oxford Dictionary of the Christian Church* (1997), s.v. "Incarnation."

Christ's incarnation served several purposes. First, Christ became man "for us . . . and our salvation" by Mary the virgin, the mother of God or human God bearer, the *theotokos*.

Second, Christ incarnate inaugurates the completion of the "God with humanity" project that began in the garden in the beginning but was derailed by sin. After sin, God resided with Israel in the tabernacle and the temple. He then came to us in Jesus Christ. He is present in the church by the Holy Spirit. Christ will come again and live with the whole company of the redeemed eternally in the new heavens and the new earth. After all, he promised, "I will never leave you nor forsake you" (Heb. 13:5).

Third, Christ's incarnation shows us what God is like. Our sin-produced inability to see or know God necessitated the incarnation in order that we might understand him. As John 1:18 states, "No one has ever seen God; the only God, who is at the Father's side [Jesus], he has made him known." Jesus explained God.

Fourth, the incarnate Christ also shows us what humanity is like. Our sin-produced inability to see or know ourselves necessitated the incarnation in order that we might understand who we are and what we are to be like. Jesus is the God-man, the theanthropic person, who instantiates a true humanity that Christians are to emulate. Christ shows us the new, true way to be human—created, judged, forgiven, and made alive in him.[19] Consequently, we have clarity about our identity amidst a spate of confusing anthropological options: Confucian, Hindu, Buddhist, Islamic, Platonic, Kantian, Marxist, Freudian, existentialist, behaviorist, pragmatist, therapeutic, modern, postmodern, and so on.

Fifth, Christ's incarnation valorizes human nature and the physical creation. Through his enfleshment, Christ declared our worth and the worth of the whole created world. "Good is the flesh that the Word has become," writes Brian Wren in his poem

---

[19] Dietrich Bonhoeffer, *Ethics*, trans. Reinhard Krauss, Charles C. West, and Douglas W. Stott, ed. Clifford J. Green (Minneapolis: Fortress, 2000), 159.

of the same title.[20] In Christ, God declares all things to be very good once again.

The incarnation of Jesus Christ has tremendous philosophic implications in reversing a multitude of deficient dualisms. In Jesus, soul and body are united, establishing human wholeness (anthropology). In him, faith and reason are reconciled, making knowledge a seamless robe (epistemology). He reunited heaven and earth, re-enchanting the world with God's presence and glory (metaphysics). He connected values and facts, generating an integral moral vision (ethics). In him, grace restores nature, making all things new (soteriology and eschatology). Humanity. Knowledge. Metaphysics. Ethics. Soteriology. Eschatology. These are just a few areas in which the incarnation fuels a Christian philosophical outlook.

## CHRISTIAN HUMANISM

A Christian anthropology culminates in a Christian humanism. As all humanisms do, Christian humanism emphasizes the dignity of people. Christian humanism has an adequate basis for believing in the value and worth of human beings in the doctrines of creation and incarnation. Other humanistic philosophies, however, lack adequate foundations to support their enthusiastic affirmations of people. Are we really all that special if the billions of us came about by evolutionary accident, behave like animals, and are heading toward oblivion or annihilation? Because it has adequate foundations, Christianity of all the humanisms, then, can make the surprising claim to be the true one.

Whereas contemporary secular humanism boasts of its reliance on human reason and is founded on scientific naturalism, a Christian humanism is derived from a canonical Trinitarian theism that is guiding us in our study of philosophy. On the same basis, a helpful document titled "A Christian Humanist Manifesto" asserts

---

[20] Brian Wren, *Advent, Christmas, and Epiphany: Liturgies and Prayers for Public Worship* (Louisville: Westminster, 2008), 137.

that the proper starting point for Christian humanism is with God and humanity together.[21] God constitutes the ultimate meaning of the universe, according to this declaration. By including him in its understanding of reality, Christian humanism avoids the reductionism of secular humanism, which limits its view of things to humankind alone. We need God and people *together*.

Christian humanism, according to this Manifesto, also entails our identity as God's image. It upholds the value of life, and envisions the purposes of human existence to be bound up in fellowship with God. It honors the tasks of creational stewardship and development and recognizes that God gives ultimate meanings to our labor and leisure, science and art, family and state, and so on.

"A Christian Humanist Manifesto" recognizes the existence of both truth and error, along with the horrific problem of evil fostered by our sinful separation from God. Nonetheless, it confidently affirms God's providence over creation, history, and human affairs. Above all, it exults in Christ's work of redemption on our behalf.

> To end our alienation from him [God] and to restore human life to its original design and purpose, our Creator has acted [redemptively] in the life, death, and resurrection of Jesus Christ, a first-century Jew who was, in truth, the second person of the Trinity, God incarnate.[22]

The kingdom of God has come in Christ, and he and the kingdom are coming again in the future to complete the work of redemption. Meanwhile, the church as the body of Christ, despite her weaknesses, carries out her many-sided, humanizing missions in the world.

Certainly, Christian humanism recognizes that the world is

---

[21] "A Christian Humanist Manifesto" first appeared as part of an article titled "Secular vs. Christian Humanism," *Eternity* (January 1982), 15–22. It is now available as an appendix in J. I. Packer and Thomas Howard, *Christianity: The True Humanism* (Vancouver: Regent College Publishing, 1999), 239–42.

[22] "Appendix on Christian Humanism," in Packer and Howard, *Christianity*, 241.

in crisis. Yet it believes that it can provide a framework for solutions to its many agonizing problems. Thus, it advocates neither an undue pessimism nor a superficial optimism about the future. Instead, it offers an appropriate Christian realism in light of the overall human condition. A "Christian Humanist Manifesto" concludes with this reminder:

> In contrast to secular humanism, therefore, Christian humanism does not hesitate to speak of absolute truth, goodness, beauty, love, morality, the sanctity of life, duty, fidelity, hope, and immortality. These are not empty religious sentiments, but the natural language of those who know even if partially, of their creation and redemption by a loving God.

Indeed, God created us in the beginning as his image with all its attendant faculties and functions. Despite our rebellion, God became man in Jesus Christ, and he has restored us to a truly human life in him. As Irenaeus said, "The glory of God is a person fully alive."[23] The more Christlike and alive we are, the more honor and recognition goes to God. Our creation as God's image and the reality of God's incarnation in Christ flow naturally in establishing the grand vision of Christian humanism, the full flowering of the incarnation of the Son of God who lived, died, rose from the dead, and is coming again.[24]

## CONCLUSION: EGOISM AND ALTRUISM

Christian philosophic principles such as these should provide a framework for engaging philosophical anthropology in creative, critical, corrective, and complementary ways. At the same time, we want to know how philosophic reflection, as a handmaiden, illuminates the meanings of Christian personhood to make its

---

[23] Irenaeus, *Against Heresies* 20.7.

[24] Thomas Merton, "Virginity and Humanism in the Western Fathers," quoted in R. William Franklin and Joseph M. Shaw, *The Case for Christian Humanism* (Grand Rapids, MI: Eerdmans, 1991), 4.

teachings clearer. Philosophical input on such issues as the existence of souls and other minds, the mind/body problem, the nature of personal identity, the matters of freedom and determinism, the question about life after death, and so on should give Christian thinkers much to consider.

Philosophic reflection on egoism and altruism, for example, has helped me to think more carefully about Christian anthropology. Are human beings naturally egotistical and selfish? Is selfishness a virtue? If selfishness is a virtue, as Ayn Rand (1905–1982) suggested, then perhaps we should choose it.[25] On the other hand, maybe we are naturally altruistic and self-giving. If not, shouldn't we at least try to be?

Philosophers who have dealt with these matters have helped me see that all our actions entail self-related benefits. Aren't we all motivated, at least in part, to help the needy because of the good feelings we experience in rendering aid? Aren't we motivated to good Christian behavior by the prospect of rewards? Didn't we believe in Christ so that we might avoid the torments of hell?

Abraham Lincoln was apparently a believer in what has become known as "psychological egoism"—that people primarily act on behalf of themselves. As an illustrative story has it, Lincoln's efforts to save a mother pig and her piglets from drowning in a rainstorm were not as selfless as they seemed: "I should have had no peace of mind all day," he confessed, "had I gone on and left that suffering old sow worrying over those piglets. I did it [saved them] to get peace of mind don't you see?"[26]

I concluded from these considerations that there can be such a thing as enlightened, Christian self-interest. To be sure, we can act in *sinfully* selfish ways. However, just because we are recompensed in some way for our service, whether now or in eternity, doesn't make us bad people. It seems to be the way God made us.

---

[25] Ayn Rand, *The Virtue of Selfishness: A New Concept of Egoism* (New York: Signet, 1964).
[26] Quoted in Robert C. Solomon and Kathleen M. Higgins, *The Big Questions: A Short Introduction to Philosophy*, 8th ed. (Belmont, CA: Wadsworth, 2010), 254.

4

# EPISTEMOLOGY

The concept of revelation must . . . yield an epistemology of its own.

—Dietrich Bonhoeffer[1]

Philosophers ask questions and think about things that most people take for granted—things such as knowledge or epistemology. What do I know? How do I know it? In this chapter, we want to learn how insights from canonical Trinitarian theism can help us configure a Christian epistemology.

"Inescapable frameworks," to use a phrase from Charles Taylor, shape our views of everything, including epistemology.[2] A Christian framework posits that God is there, that he is not silent, and that we humans are his image and likeness. This kind of Christian framework is very significant when it comes to knowledge.[3] On the other hand, a naturalistic framework denies that God is there and says that silence is all there is and that we humans are advanced primates and nothing more. This kind of naturalistic framework has unavoidable consequences for epistemology. Christianity and naturalism, respectively, have enormous epistemological implications. "Nothing less than being human is at stake."[4]

Of course, we are not talking about whether we can understand the little, "easy to know" things in life (such as the content

[1] Dietrich Bonhoeffer, *Act and Being: Transcendental Philosophy and Ontology in Systematic Theology*, ed. Wayne Whitson Floyd Jr., trans. H. Martin Rumscheidt, vol. 2 of *Dietrich Bonhoeffer Works*, ed. Wayne Whitson Floyd (Minneapolis: Fortress, 1996), 31.

[2] Charles Taylor, *Sources of the Self: The Making of Modern Identity* (Cambridge, MA: Harvard University Press, 1989), 3.

[3] I am alluding to Francis Schaeffer's book *He Is There and He Is Not Silent* (Wheaton, IL: Tyndale, 1972).

[4] Bonhoeffer, *Act and Being*, 30.

of the label on a soup can). Rather, we are concerned about our knowledge of the big, "tough to know" stuff such as the meaning of life—God, humanity, knowledge, ethics, beauty, and so on. The magnitude of the issues makes it all the more necessary to find our way knowledge-*wise*.

## EPISTEMIC MIASMA

We live in cultures and go to churches enveloped in dense, epistemic fog. To change the metaphor, it's an epistemological jungle out there. Truth and knowing it have become the paramount issues of our times. All too often, however, we confuse good and evil, light and darkness, or, metaphorically, the bitter and the sweet (Isa. 5:20–21). We profess intelligence and wisdom, but we're idiots (Rom. 1:22). Either the media serves as our basic epistemology or we subscribe, willy-nilly, to an atheistic or naturalistic worldview with its evolutionary development of the human person without recognizing the epistemic implications.

In regard to "media as epistemology," critic Neil Postman (1931–2003) believed that American culture had reached a critical point in the mid 1980s as the electronic world had unwaveringly altered our symbolic or cognitive environment. TV was his major concern. "We are now a culture," he wrote, "whose information, ideas and epistemology are given form by television."[5] Of course, Postman's observation predated the Internet, social media, and an array of e-gadgetry that now serve as unsuspected epistemological instruments. Through various media, popular culture and entertainment reign in epistemology. Countless celebrities are our teachers.

In naturalistic evolutionary theory, survival is the goal of the developmental process. It entails adaptation, competition, and cooperation among species in demanding environments. What

---

[5] Neil Postman, *Amusing Ourselves to Death: Public Discourse in the Age of Show Business* (New York: Penguin, 1985), 28.

epistemic implications might survivalism have in the formation of various human cognitive capacities? Many think it would eliminate any concern for truth or truthfulness (except by accident) in the human evolutionary process. Endurance would be the primary desideratum rather than truth. Furthermore, if humans are merely advanced primates, do we (or they) have any good reasons to trust the ideas in our (their) minds? Blind evolutionary development of human cognition casts appropriate doubts on evolution itself and the metaphysical naturalism that undergirds it.

Charles Darwin worried about this in a letter to W. Graham, dated July 3, 1881: "But then with me the horrid doubt always arises whether the convictions of man's mind, which has developed from the mind of the lower animals, are of any value or at all trustworthy. Would anyone trust the convictions of a monkey's mind, if there are any convictions in such a mind?"[6] Hence, a naturalistic evolutionism, ironically, could be epistemically incoherent.

Naturalism could, in fact, render naturalism itself irrational, as Alvin Plantinga argues, and as C. S. Lewis thought. Plantinga devotes chapter 12 of his work *Warrant and Proper Function* to this point.[7] He writes in one place that "if metaphysical naturalism and this evolutionary account are both true, then our cognitive faculties will have resulted from blind mechanisms like natural selection. . . . Evolution is interested, not in true belief, but in survival or fitness. It is therefore unlikely that our cognitive faculties have the production of true belief as a proximate or any other function, and the probability of our faculties being reliable (given naturalistic evolution) would be fairly low."[8] If, then, naturalism negates knowing, then theism fosters it. Our native human capacity to know, Plantinga claims, "flourishes best in the

---

[6] Charles Darwin, *The Autobiography of Charles Darwin and Selected Letters*, ed. Francis Darwin (New York: Dover, 1892; repr. 1958), 67.
[7] Alvin Plantinga, *Warrant and Proper Function* (New York: Oxford University Press, 1993), 216–37.
[8] Ibid., 219.

context of supernaturalism in metaphysics."[9] I agree. So did C. S. Lewis.[10] From this, we see why God must underwrite a credible epistemology.

## SPECIAL AND NATURAL REVELATION

The world presents itself to us as a question to be answered. We are also mysteries to ourselves and others and need a little input, to put it mildly, to figure ourselves and others out. Human reason has clearly shown itself to be enfeebled and tired, incapable of understanding the riddles of life. As Augustine offered rather poetically, "But when we come to divine things, this faculty [of reason] turns away; it cannot behold; it pants, it gasps, and burns with desire; it falls back from the light of truth, and turns again to its wonted [customary] obscurity, not from choice, but from exhaustion."[11] We best not lean on our own understanding, as Proverbs 3:5 instructs. Otherwise, we might be blind to our own blindness.[12]

In light of our fatigue and failure to offer a credible conception of the tough-to-know stuff, we need God's help. We need to be told by him what is true. We must then submit humbly to his revealed declarations. After all, if God can form the mountains and create the wind, he can also declare to us what are his thoughts (Amos 4:13). From a basis of trust in God's revelation, philosophic understanding ensues. We have a revealed faith seeking understanding.

Direct, face-to-face communication with God was the original epistemic arrangement. However, our rebellion changed all that. The noetic and cardiac effects of sin were and are titanic. In

---

[9] Ibid., ix.

[10] C. S. Lewis, Miracles: A Preliminary Study (New York: Macmillan, 1947), 22.

[11] Augustine, On the Morals of the Catholic Church, trans. Richard Stothert, vol. 4 of Nicene and Post-Nicene Fathers, First Series, ed. Philip Schaff (Peabody, MA: Hendrickson, 1994), 44.

[12] John Montag, SJ, "Revelation: The False Legacy of Suarez," in Radical Orthodoxy: A New Theology, ed. John Milbank, Catherine Pickstock, and Graham Ward (New York: Routledge, 1999), 38.

a fallen world, pervasive ignorance and wrong desire plague us. Now God graciously speaks to us *indirectly* through the signs and symbols of his inspired Word (2 Tim. 3:16–17). How else would we know anything at all? "For the Bible tells me so" is an epistemologically significant phrase.

God's written Word of revelation—the Bible—is, nevertheless, mysterious in its composition. Though it is God's Word, it is also of human authorship (forty-plus authors). Like the incarnate Christ, Scripture is fully human and fully divine. He was a *theanthropic* person. The Bible is a *theanthropic* book. Like the authority of the living Word, God's written Word possesses the same infallibility regarding its instructions on Christian faith and practice.

Though Scripture as a sacred text has competitors in its claim to revelation, its content is self-authenticating. It contains the seeds of its own justification, especially as its truth is confirmed by "the secret testimony of the Holy Spirit"—*testimonium internum Spiritus Sancti*.[13] Indeed, the Holy Spirit is the Spirit of truth. He abides within believers, teaches us the truth, and enables us to remember Jesus's words (John 14:17, 26). He testifies to our minds, hearts, and spirits that the Bible and the faith it proclaims are true. This is a Spirit-shaped apologetic, though we may certainly use other methods to vouchsafe the faith's authenticity. Regardless, "our full persuasion and assurance of the infallible truth and divine authority . . . [of Scripture are] from the inward work of the Holy Spirit bearing witness by and with the Word in our hearts."[14]

The modernist knowledge structures we are familiar with (fixed, atomistic, scientific, specialized, detached, etc.) must be replaced by an epistemology arising from Scripture.[15] The

---

[13] John Calvin, *Institutes of the Christian Religion*, ed. John T. McNeill, trans. Ford Lewis Battles, vol. 22 of The Library of Christian Classics, ed. John Baillie, John T. McNeill, Henry P. Van Dusen (Philadelphia: Westminster, 1960), 1.7.4.
[14] Westminster Confession of Faith (1646), 1.5.
[15] Joel B. Green, "The (Re-)Turn to Narrative," in *Narrative Reading, Narrative Preaching: Reuniting New Testament Interpretation and Proclamation*, ed. Joel B. Green and Michael Psaquarello III (Grand Rapids, MI: Baker Academic, 2003), 20.

Spirit-inspired and validated Bible, as if it were a pair of glasses, clarifies our feeble and scattered vision of God (and everything else), as John Calvin's familiar illustration helps us to understand:

> Just as old bleary-eyed men and those with weak vision, if you thrust before them a beautiful volume, even if they recognize it to be some sort of writing, yet can scarcely construe two words, but with the aid of spectacles will begin to read distinctly; so Scripture, gathering up the otherwise confused knowledge of God in our minds, having dispersed our dullness, clearly shows us the true God.[16]

Of course, Scripture as spectacles declares all its truths from the vantage point of redemption. If we are the beneficiaries of Christ's salvation, then from the whole counsel of God in Scripture we discover truths about the cosmos. We learn that God exists and is the creator, judge, and redeemer of the world. We also learn from this same inscripturated source that creation reveals God's truth and glory to everyone, everywhere. This is called natural or general revelation since, respectively, it comes through creation and is available to all. Thus we study and learn from both the book of Scripture and the book of nature. We learn what the latter (the book of nature) really is from the former (the book of Scripture), and when both are correctly interpreted (something only God can really do), they agree in content and application.

In redemptive perspective, therefore, natural or general revelation is an epistemic treasure trove. All our scientific, educational, and philosophic endeavors have the potential to inform us about the whole of God's reality, assuming we have eyes to see and ears to hear. Sometimes I think there is as much insight to be gleaned from general revelation as there is from special revelation.

---

[16] Calvin, *Institutes of the Christian Religion*, 1.6.1.

## KNOWLEDGE AND NARRATIVES

We are narrative creatures (*homo narrativus*). Our lives are a story. We also live our lives in the context of some larger, all-encompassing tale about life and the world. Some narrative that is greater than ourselves provides the plot or plots we are following. These larger stories come from a variety of sources, especially the media and science.

Of course, God has a story, and it's in the Bible. We've been calling it "canonical Trinitarian theism." We are to subordinate our personal micro-narratives to God's larger macro-narrative, which supplies us with meaning and perspective. Christian philosophers who have adopted this story as their own are to philosophize on its basis, since it contains significant metaphysical, anthropological, epistemological, ethical, and aesthetic insights. Faith in God's story prompts us to seek philosophic understanding of these things.

The biblical story is epistemologically weighty in several ways. First, it is world informing in its settings, characters, conflicts, drama, plot, and resolution. Second, it stimulates our imaginations and prompts us to consider things in a fresh light. Third, it encourages personal engagement as we envisage ourselves as characters in the drama and recognize the implications of our participation. Fourth, it motivates us to action as we grasp its practical, world-changing import. Fifth and finally, the biblical story has profound ethical implications. It tells us what to be and do. Some of us probably need to be re-narrated.

There is an incredulity toward metanarratives these days.[17] Even so, they still abound. They are an inescapable trait of human beings who live by faith in their big stories. These stories come to us through the media and other sources (home, church, school, government). Though they are plentiful and of different content, they can be summarized under three headings: the narratives of

---

[17] Jean-François Lyotard, *The Postmodern Condition: A Report on Knowledge*, trans. Geoff Bennington and Brian Massumi (Minneapolis: University of Minnesota Press, 1984), *xxiv*.

*sensualism* (sex, food, fashion), *materialism* (money, wealth, possessions), and *egotism* (achievement, prestige, power). In biblical language, these three stories are the three themes of the lust of the flesh, the lust of the eyes, and the boastful pride of life (1 John 2:16). Most people live their lives in accordance with one of these three basic plots (or in combination). If lived consistently, the practical results of these stories can be profound. But are they the true stories? What is the world's true story? Has it been lost?[18] The world's true story, which has been lost, is about God and creation, humanity and sin, Jesus and redemption. This biblical story ought to become the "habitual texture of the mind" for Christian philosophers,[19] who should find their identities and roles and the wherewithal of their thought and service in this dramatic context.

## KNOWLEDGE AND EMBODIED LOVE

We love our stories, and, all things being equal, we will typically seek to know something about whatever it is we care about most deeply. It's a natural connection. "I'd love to know" is more than just an idle phrase. Sports enthusiasts, for example, typically want to know more about their favorite pastime. Love a book or books? Love a person? Love God? Our loves may even lead to a college major and a career. As Esther Meek says, "The central and shaping motive of knowing is love."[20] In other words, our loves, even if they are subterranean, beget and direct our knowing.

Furthermore, as our loves change, so will our epistemic pursuits. New affections and desires will displace old ones as time passes, and a quest for new insights follows fresh interests. There is an integral connection, then, between "knowledge and human interests."[21]

---

[18] I am alluding to Robert W. Jenson's "How the World Lost Its Story," *First Things* (October 1993): 19–24.
[19] Bernard Lonergan, *Insight*, vol. 3 of *Collected Works of Bernard Lonergan*, ed. Frederick E. Crowe and Robert M. Doran (Toronto: University of Toronto Press, 1992), 28.
[20] Esther Lightcap Meek, *Loving to Know: Covenant Epistemology* (Eugene, OR: Cascade, 2011), 428.
[21] Jürgen Habermas, *Knowledge and Human Interests*, trans. Jeremy J. Shapiro (Boston: Beacon Press, 1971).

Modern epistemology sought to divorce head and heart. However, thinking and feeling are allies, not enemies. Scientists have even shown neurologically that emotion is necessary for reason to function. There is also evidence that emotions can be reasonable and reason can be emotional in an emotional rationality or in a rational emotionality. Of course, there are major epistemological and practical implications for this conjunction.

The connection between knowing and loving can be a good or a bad thing, depending on the character of our loves as the prime movers of knowledge. If our loves are out of kilter, chances are that our knowing will be also. If we wish to get our knowing in good order, we'd better work on our loves. Paul is spot on in writing these words to the church at Philippi: "It is my prayer that your love may abound more and more, *with knowledge and all discernment*" (Phil. 1:9).

One of the chief consequences of Christian redemption is a vast reordering of our deepest loves. We move from disordered loves to transformed ones. The sanctification of the loves and desires of our hearts has to be one of the greatest miracles of all. As Bernard Lonergan has pointed out, redemption "dismantles and abolishes the horizon in which our knowing and choosing went on and it sets up a new horizon in which the love of God will transvaluate our values and the eyes of that love will transform our knowing."[22] Paul conveys a similar idea in 1 Corinthians 1:5, where he recognizes that believers in Jesus are enriched "in all speech and all knowledge."

We must also point out that these loves and desires of ours are embodied. Indeed, we should affirm that knowledge, story, and affection are embodied realities and not just nonphysical ones. Not only do we process things with our minds and emotions, but we also apprehend reality with our senses by what we see, hear, taste, touch, and smell. They tell us significant things about visual, audible, tasty, feely, and smelly realities.

As embodied beings, we also occupy particular places, associate

---

[22] Bernard Lonergan, *Method in Theology* (New York: Herder & Herder, 1972), 106.

with particular people, experience particular events, and learn about particular things. We participate as embodied beings in various rituals that have shaped us inside out and outside in. We are always entwined within a particular network of determinants—beliefs, powers, concerns, and so on. Where we have lived, the people with whom we have lived, the things we have done and that have been done to us, and the customs and traditions to which we have been exposed have had decisive impact. In other words, our knowledge of God, self, others, and the world has been environmentally, sociologically, historically, and culturally situated and shaped because we are embodied beings who, presumably, dwell in the world heedfully, circumspectly, and essentially.[23] In short, we have bodies of knowledge.

## DIALECTIC BETWEEN THEORY AND PRACTICE

How do we learn and come to know? Do we come to know through ritualized behaviors from which intuitions and truth surface? Or do we begin with the mind and ideas which then leverage experience? Is the apprehension of ideas from the bottom up or the top down, so to speak? In liturgical terms, the issue is whether prayer and worship give rise to belief, or whether belief gives rise to prayer and worship. Furthermore, how might all three—prayer, worship, and belief—shape action? Is it *Lex orandi est lex credendi et agendi*, that is, the law of prayer is the law of belief and action,[24] or is it *Lex credendi est lex orandi et agendi*, that is, the law of belief is the law of prayer and action?[25] Which comes first, in other words: prayer or belief?

A historical materialist would say that ideas originate from the bottom up: conditions form consciousness. A cultural idealist, on the other hand, would argue that ideas are first conceived

---

[23] Martin Heidegger, *Being and Time*, trans. Joan Stambaugh (Albany: State University of New York Press, 2010), 116.
[24] Attributed to Pope Coelestinus or Celestine I (422–432). See Richard A. Muller, *Dictionary of Latin and Greek Theological Terms: Drawn Principally from Protestant Scholastic Theology* (Grand Rapids, MI: Baker, 1985), 175.
[25] Geoffrey Wainwright, *Doxology: The Praise of God in Worship, Doctrine, and Life* (New York: Oxford University Press, 1984), chaps. 7–8, esp. pp. 218–19, 251–52.

and then thrust upon life and the world from above: consciousness forms conditions. Perhaps it's both, like a dance among factors, in which one leads on one occasion and another on another. We learn both ways, dialectically.[26]

For me, ideas have arisen from praxis, but my praxis has also been informed and formed by ideas. For example, I intuited much from my experiences as an administrator in adult education. However, I did not understand it very well until I read, reflected, and wrote about it theoretically. If nothing else, there is an epistemological reciprocity of ideas and experience. Both should be consummated in constructive action.

## CONCLUSION: THE NATURE OF KNOWLEDGE

These ideas, among many others, can help Christian philosophers engage various epistemological issues in creative, critical, corrective, and complementary ways. Those issues include the possibility of knowledge (agnosticism, skepticism, idols of the mind), the sources of knowledge (reason, experience, intuition, testimony, pragmatism), the nature of knowledge (as justified true belief, objective, subjective), theories and tests for truth (correspondence, coherence, pragmatic perspectives), the justification of knowledge (strong and weak foundationalism, coherentism and contextualism), science, knowledge, and faith, how well we know or don't know life and the world (naive realism, critical realism, creative anti-realism), and the connection between virtue and epistemology. Additionally, normal philosophic reflection—the handmaiden— on these and many other questions will undoubtedly contribute to a Christian understanding of knowledge and stimulate considerable creative thought and practice.

In any case, let me suggest how an epistemology born of canonical Trinitarian theism can critique and correct the modern idea of

---

[26] Paul L. Gavrilyuk, "Canonical Liturgies: The Dialectic of *Lex Orandi* and *Lex Credendi*," in *Canonical Theism: A Proposal for Theology and the Church*, ed. William J. Abraham, Jason E. Vickers, Natalie B. Van Kirk (Grand Rapids, MI: Eerdmans, 2008), 61–72.

knowledge as "scientifically derived data, facts and information."[27] Though some of its assertions are rooted in history and subject to empirical verification, the Bible's account of knowledge is much richer in character than those on offer today. Here are some interconnected reasons why.

First, knowledge is personal. Truth is a person (God), and knowledge of the truth is knowledge of a person and, thus, personal. The implication is that we should know God and people, as well as places and things, in personal ways. In brief, we are to know all things (personally) as we are known.[28]

Second, knowledge is relational. We enter intimately into a relationship with God and people and the places and things we seek to apprehend. Interestingly, both the Hebrew and Greek words for knowledge (respectively, *yada* and *ginōskō*) are used euphemistically in Scripture of sexual intercourse (see Gen. 4:1; Matt. 1:25). On this basis, we can claim that regular knowledge is equally relational. Consequently, it is also characterized by love, care, concern, and responsibility. Enthusiastic teachers demonstrate this kind of intimacy with their subjects, even if it's with inanimate things such as numbers or genes.

Third, knowledge is covenantal. True knowers are obligated to put their knowledge into practice, regardless of the realm they claim to know. Knowers have serious responsibilities to observe what they have apprehended or been apprehended by (e.g., Deut. 6:17; Matt. 7:24–27). In Mark Schwehn's words, "ways of knowing are not morally neutral but morally directive."[29]

When we put all this together, we realize there is more to human knowing than human knowing will ever know.[30]

[27] Mary Hesse, *Revolutions and Reconstructions in the Philosophy of Science* (Indianapolis: Indiana University Press, 1980), *vii.*
[28] See Parker J. Palmer, *To Know As We Are Known: A Spirituality of Education* (New York: HarperCollins, 1983).
[29] Mark R. Schwehn, *Exiles from Eden: Religion and the Academic Vocation in America* (New York: Oxford University Press, 1993), 94.
[30] Os Guinness, *In Two Minds: The Dilemma of Doubt and How to Resolve It* (Downers Grove, IL: InterVarsity, 1976), 41.

# ✚ 5

# ETHICS

Therefore . . . how should we then live?

—Ezekiel 33:10 (KJV)

Philosophers ask questions and think about things that most people take for granted, things such as ethics or moral philosophy. Admittedly, people are more interested in the ethical realm than they are in the other philosophic subdisciplines considered in this volume. It's probably because of the relevance of the questions asked. What is right and wrong? Who is a good (not just a nice) person? How should we then live? In this chapter, we want to understand how insights from canonical Trinitarian theism can help us gain a Christian ethical outlook.

In an old *Calvin and Hobbes* cartoon (1993), Calvin contemplated whether he should cheat on a test at school. Seeking a way to justify his cheating, Calvin tells Hobbes that in the real world, people care about *success, not principles.* He immediately wonders, however, if this ethical approach is why the world is in such a mess. In thinking about this dilemma, he ended up turning in a blank paper, since, as he concluded, "It just seemed wrong to cheat on an ethics test."[1]

Ethics is a subdivision of axiology (the study of things of worth and value). Aesthetics also fits in this category as the examination of artistic values (see the next chapter). Both ethics and aesthetics, then, belong in the axiological class.

---

[1] Bill Waterston, *There's Treasure Everywhere—A Calvin and Hobbes Collection* (Kansas City, MO: Andrews and McMeel, 1996), 12.

In the history of philosophy among the Greeks, many wanted to know what was metaphysically real, anthropologically genuine, and epistemologically true in order that they might do the ethical good. "In what way should one live one's life?" was the primary concern.[2] Ethics, in other words, was the end game of philosophy.[3]

"Inescapable frameworks" shape our views of ethics like they do everything else. For example, if there's a God, morality is drawn in. If there isn't, morality is affected. God's existence or the lack thereof is ethically determinative. To put it metaphorically, our frameworks tell us if there are red lights and green lights that govern the moral traffic of human affairs. If there are, where do these "lights" come from? Is everyone aware of them? The belief that there is an inborn sense of right and wrong is called natural law.

## ETHICS AND NATURAL LAW

Indeed, we all have basic moral sensibilities. Natural law posits that these dispositions are standard equipment. For example, we have an innate sense of love and also of fair play or giving others their due. Since these sentiments are natural, we really don't need in-depth teaching about what to be and do when it comes to matters of love and justice—two of the most prominent concepts in the moral cultures of the world.[4]

Tart responses to hatred and injustice, especially if we are the victims, seem to disclose an inherent set of moral motions and notions within. Who doesn't recoil at overt expressions of animosity? Who doesn't vociferously protest an apparent evaluative injustice? Who tolerates malicious deception? Along these lines, Augustine once reported, "I have met many who wished to

[2] Plato (Socrates), *Gorgias*, trans. W. C. Helmbold (New York: Macmillan, 1952), 73.
[3] I owe this thought to Mark Sadler.
[4] Nicholas Wolterstorff, *Love in Justice* (Grand Rapids, MI: Eerdmans, 2011), *vii*. See also his *Justice: Rights and Wrongs* (Princeton, NJ: Princeton University Press, 2007).

deceive, but not one who wished to be deceived."[5] In other words, we will lie to others, but we certainly don't want others to lie to us.

C. S. Lewis was a recent defender of the natural law tradition.[6] He saw the innate sense of "Right and Wrong as a clue to the meaning of the universe." As he declared, "Human beings, all over the earth, have this curious idea that they ought to behave in a certain way, and cannot really get rid of it."[7]

From what sources does this inborn sense of morality come? Ultimately it comes from the God of the Scriptures. The *locus classicus* for natural law is found in Paul's epistle to the Romans:

> For when Gentiles, who do not have the law, by nature do what the law requires, they are a law to themselves, even though they do not have the law. *They show that the work of the law is written on their hearts*, while their conscience also bears witness, and their conflicting thoughts accuse or even excuse them on that day when, according to my gospel, God judges the secrets of men by Christ Jesus. (2:14–16)

In a rhetorically strategic move in *The Abolition of Man*, Lewis used the Chinese word *Tao* (the way, path, route) to refer to the law written on the heart.[8] After a defense of the concept in the three chapters of the book, he offers illustrations of the *Tao* in an appendix. There he cites laws of general and specific beneficence, duties to parents, elders, ancestors, children, and posterity, and laws of justice, good faith, veracity, mercy, and magnanimity. All these examples came from ready-to-hand sources that Lewis said merely provided anecdotal evidence for the natural law. Regardless, he believed that to disallow the *Tao* would be to bury

---

[5] Augustine, *Confessions*, trans F. J. Sheed (Indianapolis: Hackett, 1993), 10.23.

[6] Of course, Thomas Aquinas is the noted Roman Catholic advocate of natural law. See his *Treatise on Law* and also his *Summa Theologica*, q. 90–97.

[7] C. S. Lewis, *Mere Christianity* (New York: Macmillan, 1958), 7.

[8] C. S. Lewis, *The Abolition of Man: Or Reflections on Education with Special Reference to the Teaching of English in the Upper Forms of Schools* (New York: HarperCollins, 2001).

education and give unbridled power to science. The loss of the *Tao* or natural law would mean the abolition of man:

> Stepping outside the *Tao*, they [human scientific conditioners] have stepped into the void. Nor are their subjects [of experiments] necessarily unhappy men. They are not men at all: they are artefacts. Man's final conquest has proved to be the abolition of man.[9]

## ETHICS AND SPECIAL REVELATION

Natural law is properly attributed to God, as his moral expectations are written naturally on the tablets of human hearts. Additionally, God has revealed his ethical commands and demands in the moral content of both the Old and New Testaments. In general, revealed biblical morality is known as *divine command ethics* insofar as moral directives are rooted in God's will and nature and proffered to those in covenant with him for their obedience.

> On a divine command conception, actions forbidden by God are morally wrong because they are thus forbidden [prohibitions such as murder], actions not forbidden by God are morally right because they are not thus forbidden [permissions such as truth telling], and actions commanded by God are morally obligatory because they are thus commanded [obligations such as love].[10]

From this, we can see that God's will and Word specify what is to be done because he has commanded it, consequences aside. As Augustine thought, God will command what he wills and will grant what he commanded.[11]

The question of whether God's laws originate in his will or essence has been the subject of considerable debate over the years. Is something right because God wills it? This view, focusing on God's will, is called "voluntarism." Or does God will something

---

[9] Ibid., 64.
[10] *Cambridge Dictionary of Philosophy*, 2nd ed., s.v. "Divine Command Ethics."
[11] Augustine, *Confessions* 10.29.

because it is right? This position, highlighting God's nature, is called "essentialism."

Advocates of voluntarism seek to uphold God's complete freedom to choose as he may. Would hatred and cruelty, then, be options? Advocates of essentialism highlight God's moral perfection, which determines his moral commands.

Is there a way of combining these two schools of thought? For example, surely the divine commandments prohibiting adultery and fornication do not apply to God himself. Hence, these commandments must stem from God's will alone. At the same time, they are a reflection of his righteous character and also come from God's understanding of human nature. Perhaps other divine laws of prohibition, permission, and obligation show forth both God's will and holiness in a synchronous way. The Scriptures, then, suggest that the divine realities of who God is and what he has chosen are the basis for the ethics revealed in Scripture and in nature (Deut. 32:3–4; Rom. 9:11). Regardless, God whispers his divine will naturally to us in our consciences, and Scripture clarifies what he expects of his people in the more clear and precise commandments of the Bible.

## VICES AND VIRTUES

Alasdair MacIntyre has taught us to recognize the narrative sources of the moral traditions to which we adhere, especially if we wish to establish coherent, unified lives. Our character and actions, he told us, are essentially "an enacted dramatic narrative." We know neither what to be or what to do unless we can answer the prior question, "Of what story or stories do I find myself a part?"[12]

Stories are of ultimate moral significance. For example, Plato's metaphysical narrative certainly supplied the decisive justification for the virtues of courage for the military, temperance

---

[12] Alasdair MacIntyre, *After Virtue: A Study in Moral Theory*, 2nd ed. (Notre Dame, IN: University of Notre Dame Press, 1984), 215–16 (and chap. 15 as a whole).

for workers, prudence for rulers, and justice in the community overall.

The metanarrative of Scripture serves this kind of ethical purpose. The Bible from beginning to end—canonical Trinitarian theism—embodies lists of vices and virtues that are commensurate with its grand story and substories and are definitive for the lives of God's covenant people in Israel and the church (Exodus 20; Deuteronomy 5; Psalm 15; Matt. 5:3–16; Gal. 5:22–23; 2 Pet. 1:5–7).

Augustine has helped us to see how our vices and virtues are functions of good and bad loves, respectively. On the one hand, from among the seven deadly sins, pride, envy, and anger reveal a disordered love for self. Sloth, avarice, gluttony, and lust show that we love laziness, money, food, and sex to excess. On the other hand, the seven cardinal virtues (faith, hope, love, courage, justice, temperance, and prudence) demonstrate that our deepest affections for God, ourselves, others, and the world have been significantly reordered.[13] This is why Augustine believed that love, rather than faith or hope, was the key sign of a person's goodness. "For when there is a question," Augustine wrote, "as to whether a man is good, one does not ask what he believes [faith], or what he hopes, but what he loves. For the man who loves aright no doubt believes and hopes aright."[14] Love, then, is ethically foundational to the virtues of faith and hope.

How are virtues formed? Socrates believed that to know the good was to do the good.[15] There may be intermediate steps, however. Aristotle argued that practice was the key to virtue formation: "Thus, in one word," he affirmed, "states [virtues or vices] arise out of like activities."[16] In other words, if we act courageously, we

---

[13] Augustine, *Of the Morals of the Catholic Church*, trans. Richard Stothert, vol. 4 of *Nicene and Post-Nicene Fathers*, First Series, ed. Philip Schaff (Peabody, MA: Hendrickson, 1994), 48. See also chaps. 22, 24, and 25.

[14] Augustine, *Enchiridion on Faith, Hope, and Love* (Washington, DC: Regnery, 1961), 135.

[15] Unless one is forced to do what is unjust. See *Gorgias* 460b-d; 509e; *Protagoras* 345e; 360d.

[16] Aristotle, *Nicomachian Ethics*, in *The Complete Works of Aristotle*, rev. Oxford translation, ed. Jonathan Barnes (Princeton, NJ: Princeton University Press, 1984), 1743.

will become courageous. If we act magnanimously, we will become magnanimous. This does, however, raise the proverbial "chicken and egg" dilemma. Do we need the virtue *first* in order to practice it? Or will practicing the unattained virtue somehow bequeath it to us?

To be sure, knowing what to do and doing it are steps in the right direction, even if these moves are ultimately insufficient to obtaining true virtue. Indeed, knowing and practicing these elements may induce only a kind of natural piety. On the other hand, the Christian faith adds considerable depth to the process of virtue formation. In the overarching context of the biblical story, *palingenesis* or "regeneration," Jesus's example, the Spirit's work, the church's worship, and the encouragement of Christian community are indispensable virtue-fostering factors that profoundly change the dispositions and actions of believing persons. The final goal, of course, is Christlikeness in head, heart, hand, thought, affection, and deed—"conformed to the image of his [God's] Son" (Rom. 8:29). In the end, we can assume that an already established set of dispositions produces concrete decisions. As Iris Murdoch's maxim has it, "At crucial moments of choice most of the business of choosing is already over."[17]

## THE GREATEST GOOD

Who's really well off? Who's got it good? These questions focus on the issue of the greatest good or the *summum bonum* as ethicists call it. They entail the matter of the meaning of life. To ask the same question in other ways, what is the end of all our means? Why are we here? What's the point of our journeys? What is the good life? Who is a truly good person?[18]

Some anchor our hope for purpose and meaning in things such as sex, money, and power. According to canonical Trinitarian theism, however, this is a colossal mistake. Many take hold of good

---

[17] Iris Murdoch, *The Sovereignty of Good* (New York: Schocken, 1971), 37.
[18] Dallas Willard puts the question of the greatest good in these terms. See his *Divine Conspiracy: Rediscovering Our Hidden Life in God* (New York: HarperCollins, 1998), 97.

things, overvalue them, and turn them into idols. Unfortunately, such choices culminate in "vanity" and "futility" as the Old Testament book of Ecclesiastes proclaims.[19] Even if we possess everything "under the sun" and are yet without God, nihilism approaches. We obtain the whole world and yet forfeit our souls.

A Christian moral philosophy affirms that God is the answer to the question about the greatest good and the meaning of life. According to canonical Trinitarian theism, God makes us well off. If we have him, we've got it good. He is the end of all our means, the reason why we are here, the point of our journeys. God is the good life and makes us good persons. On the other hand, to be God*less* connects to restlessness and anxiety. Augustine's famous words from the opening of his *Confessions* say it best: "O Lord, you have made us for yourself, and our hearts are restless until they rest in you." Of course, rest in and a supreme love for God do not undermine taking great delight in God's creation and its creatures. The key is learning to love both the Creator and the creation aright at the very same time.[20]

Obviously, these questions also concern genuine beatitude or happiness, not in a paltry sense but in the deep sense of the word. What is happiness? How do we obtain it? Who is truly happy? The Greeks were certainly concerned about this matter, as was Augustine. "St. Augustine's ethic," Frederick Copleston writes, "has this in common with what one might call the typical Greek ethic, that it is eudaemonistic in character, that it proposes an end for human conduct, namely happiness; but [for Augustine] this happiness is to be found in God only."[21]

While questions about the greatest good are Greek and Augustinian in character, they are also biblical. "The kingdom of

---

[19] See Peter Kreeft's insightful comments on Ecclesiastes in his *Three Philosophies of Life: Ecclesiastes: Life as Vanity, Job: Life as Suffering, Song of Songs: Life as Love* (San Francisco: Ignatius Press, 1989).
[20] David K. Naugle, *Reordered Love, Reordered Lives: Learning the Deep Meaning of Happiness* (Grand Rapids, MI: Eerdmans, 2008), 22.
[21] Frederick Copleston, SJ, *A History of Philosophy*, vol. 2 (New York: Image Books, 1962), 81.

heaven," says Jesus in Matthew 13:44, "is like treasure hidden in a field, which a man found and covered up. Then in his joy he goes and sells all that he has and buys that field." Nothing is worth more, in other words, than the kingdom of heaven. Get it, no matter the cost. Jesus says the same thing in Matthew 13:45–46: "Again, the kingdom of heaven is like a merchant in search of fine pearls, who, on finding one pearl of great value, went and sold all that he had and bought it." God and his rule are the *summum bonum*.

Those who have the treasure or pearl of God and his kingdom are happy, since it is the greatest good. Those who do not have God's kingdom are actually miserable (despite appearances) since it is the greatest good. To be truly happy, then, we must have and love what is the very best for us, as Augustine explains:

> But the title happy cannot, in my opinion, belong either [1] to him who has not what he loves, whatever it may be, or [2] to him who has what he loves if it is hurtful, or [3] to him who does not love what he has, although it is good in perfection.[22]

In the first case, how can we be happy if we don't have what we love, regardless of its identity? In the second scenario, how could we be happy if we have what we love, but what we love is not good for us? In the third situation, how could we be happy if we have what is good for us, but we don't love it? These are excellent *categories* and *distinctions*—traits of good philosophy. Augustine continues by explaining why people in these three settings cannot be happy: "For the one who seeks what he cannot obtain suffers *torture*, and one who has got what is not desirable is *cheated*, and one who does not seek what is worth seeking for is *diseased*."[23] Anybody know any people who are happy if they are tortured, cheated, or diseased? Unlikely.

Can anyone, then, be happy? Augustine envisions a fourth

---

[22] Augustine, "Of the Morals of the Catholic Church," 42.
[23] Ibid (emphasis added).

estate in which true happiness consists: ". . . when that which is man's chief good is both loved and possessed."[24] For Augustine, then, to be happy, we must know what the greatest good is, have it in our lives, and love it sincerely. Of course, according to Augustine's understanding, God is the chief good to be possessed and loved. He is the basis for good and happy lives. This is an ethical vision that is counter to any culture.

## NONCONSEQUENTIALISM AND CONSEQUENTIALISM

Results-oriented moralities are called "teleologies" and "consequentialisms." Rule-oriented moralities are "deontologies" or "nonconsequentialisms." For the former group, the morality of an action is determined by its results or consequences. If something "worked," it was right. For the latter, discovering and following the rule governing a situation, regardless of outcomes, determine the morality of an action. What's right is right, and we ought to do our duty, no matter what, even if others choose otherwise. For example, should a doting father turn in his beloved daughter to the authorities for vehicular manslaughter? Would it ever be right to lie to save an innocent life?

Consequentialists such as egoists, utilitarians, pragmatists, and situationalists would probably act practically to protect the daughter from any legal ramifications of accidentally causing the death of another. They would also probably lie to save a life. On the other hand, nonconsequentialists would insist on strict obedience to moral laws, even if it is personally costly. For example, Immanuel Kant would ask whether harboring a fugitive, even if she is a close relative, could ever be willed to become a universal law. What about lying to save a life?

What is the moral vision of Scripture? How might biblical faith affect discussions like these? Scripture seems to promote a rather rigorous nonconsequentialism with rare exceptions. Biblical

---

morality is, generally speaking, apodictic (sure and certain), attended by occasional casuistry (case analysis). More often than not, a biblical requirement is simply to be obeyed, end of story:

> Honor your father and your mother.
> You shall not murder.
> You shall not commit adultery.
> You shall not steal.
> You shall not bear false witness against your neighbor.
> You shall not covet. (See Ex. 20:12–17)

Within a narrative context of the older covenant, the general principle was this: "You shall follow my rules and keep my statutes and walk in them. I am the LORD your God" (Lev. 18:4). In the New Testament, the ethical pattern is essentially the same. Believers are to do "the will of God from the heart," which includes obeying exhortations such as those found in Ephesians 4:25–32. After all, the kingdom of God in Jesus has come and is coming. Eschatology and kingdom theology frame New Testament ethics.

While most of biblical morality is apodictic in nature, there were certain circumstances in which it appears as if God's moral laws were temporarily suspended, but for a clear purpose. The sacrifice of Isaac (Genesis 22), the lying of the Hebrew midwives (Exodus 1), the mendacity of Rahab the harlot (Joshua 2), and the civil disobedience of the first apostles (Acts 4–5) are all cases in point. Søren Kierkegaard believed that the sacrifice of Isaac entailed "the teleological suspension of the ethical," and perhaps this notion should be applied, casuistically, to these other biblical examples as well. Conceivably, the instances of Corrie Ten Boom (1892–1983), who illegally sheltered Jews in Nazi Germany in the early 1940s, and Dietrich Bonhoeffer, who conspired to assassinate Adolf Hitler—the Valkyrie plot—update these biblical scenarios and reinvigorate the claims of Christian casuistry without any ambition to foster moral laxity.

## ANTINOMIANISM

*Antinomianism* can mean either "against or without law" (*nomos* is the Greek word for "law"). The word has several meanings, but I am using it here to refer to an ethical position of relativism and general lawlessness. Some antinomians actually believe in the existence of a moral law but actively oppose it. Others disbelieve in the existence of moral law and are either *happy* about it or *resigned* to live without it. People in this second group may rejoice in or regret the absence of moral law, whereas the first group may bemoan its presence. In either case, whether in joy or sorrow, both groups seek to live *autonomously* of any law other than those of their own choosing rather than *heteronomously*, in subservience to the laws of another. Personal freedom is either the condition or goal of antinomians.

In most cases, antinomianism implies atheism (or at least any ultimate metaphysical reality that could impose red lights or green lights on us). If there is no God, there are no moral laws; if there are no moral laws, then there is likely no God. In light of God's absence and the moral law, Jean-Paul Sartre remorsefully said that human beings were condemned to freedom:

> Existentialists . . . find it extremely disturbing that God no longer exists, for along with his disappearance goes the possibility of finding values in an intelligible heaven. There could no longer be any *a priori* good, since there would be no infinite and perfect consciousness to conceive of it. Nowhere is it written that good exists, that we must be honest or must not lie, since we are on a plane shared only by men. Dostoevsky once wrote: "If God did not exist, everything is permissible." This is the starting point of existentialism.[25]

For Sartre, then, God's existence was the central issue for humanity and for ethics. God's death distressed him, for he recognized

---

[25] Jean-Paul Sartre, *Existentialism Is a Humanism*, trans. Carol Macomber (New Haven, CT: Yale University Press, 2007), 28–29.

that if God was dead, then morality was too. In a very real sense, then, Sartre was asking whether morality needs God.

In this vein, Sartre followed in Friedrich Nietzsche's wake. The latter led an all-out attack on traditional Judeo-Christian morality. For Nietzsche, God was dead, so why be good? Iconoclast though he was, Nietzsche also feared that tidal waves of nihilism would inundate the Western world in light of God's demise. What could be done to stem the forthcoming tide? Nietzsche proposed a transvaluation of all values since, in his mind, the received traditions were confining and dehumanizing. He encouraged people to break away from the weaknesses and manipulations of the herd and become powerful in self-expression, making life itself an authentic work of art. He ensconced these ideals of rebellion, strength, and creativity in what he referred to as dynamic super-humans or *Übermenschen*.

Nietzsche was a prophet, albeit an ineffective one. He was accurate in his prognostications, but his prescriptions did little to thwart the atrocities of the twentieth century. Moral relativism won the day, and the results have been horrific. We are "after virtue," indifferent to moral concerns, and have become numb to moral failure. Very little shocks us today. Only tolerance is tolerated. Only intolerance is intolerable. It must be true, then, that "the morality we are familiar with has roots in the Christian faith, and it starts to break down when its Christian context is removed."[26] The Christian context is now gone it seems. We live in a *post-Christian* society.[27] What could be more morally decisive than whether the infinite, personal, Trinitarian God of Scripture is there?

## CONCLUSION: CHRISTIAN MORAL KNOWLEDGE

Of what does a Christian moral philosophy consist? What is its substance, and how might it foster creative, critical, corrective,

---

[26] John Hare, *Why Bother Being Good? The Place of God in the Moral Life* (Downers Grove, IL: InterVarsity, 2002), 7.
[27] C. S. Lewis, "De Descriptione Temporum," in *Selected Literary Essays*, ed. Walter Hooper (Cambridge, UK: Cambridge University Press, 1969), 5.

and complementary interaction with other strains of moral philosophy? Among scores of issues to be considered, one of the biggest is about the existence of moral knowledge. Do we have it? Do we just possess person-relative values but no objective moral facts? Christian philosophy would be critical of the negation of genuine moral knowledge, whatever the reasons why. It would be creative in declaring, defining, and defending it. Dallas Willard believes this to be a kingpin issue and has tackled it in his book *Knowing Christ Today*. His central concern is "the cultural calamity of displacing the central points of Christian knowledge into the domain of mere 'faith,' sentiment, traditional ritual, or power."[28] Willard's central thesis is that faith and reason are not adversaries and that there are good reasons for trusting faith-based knowledge as we would any other. On this foundation, values are factual and facts are based on values. We have answers to the questions about how we should then live. In the end let us not forget that

> Conduct has the loudest tongue. . . .
> In the deed / The unequivocal authentic deed /
> We find sound argument, we read the heart.[29]

---

[28] Dallas Willard, *Knowing Christ Today: Why We Can Trust Spiritual Knowledge* (New York: HarperCollins, 2009), 132. For various voices on this topic, see *Moral Knowledge? New Readings in Moral Epistemology*, ed. Walter Sinnott-Armstrong and Mark Timmons (New York: Oxford University Press, 1996).

[29] William Cowper, "The Task," Book 5, *The Winter Morning Walk*, lines 650–54.

# ✚ 6

# AESTHETICS

> As the image-bearers of God, human beings
> have the ability both to create something
> beautiful and to delight in it.
>
> —Abraham Kuyper[1]

Philosophers ask questions and think about things that most people take for granted, things such as aesthetics, beauty, and philosophy of art. What is an aesthetic experience? Must art be beautiful? What is beauty anyway? In this chapter, we want to understand how insights from canonical Trinitarian theism can help us arrange a Christian aesthetic and philosophy of art.

The word *aesthetics* comes from a Greek word that means "to feel, sense, or perceive." Anyone who has been to the dentist and had an *anesthetic* grasps the literal meaning of the term. Also, at the center of the word *aesthetics* is the Greek root *the* or *thea*, which means "to see, view or look at." It's found in the English words *theory* and *theater*—and *aesthetics*. Theoreticians, theatergoers, and aestheticians are all perceivers—seers, viewers, and lookers. In philosophy the term is used of a subdiscipline that addresses questions about beauty, art, taste, and our experiences related to these matters. As a label for this philosophic domain, it is of relatively recent origin (1735).[2] Yet aesthetic concerns and questions have been with us all along. We are rightly named *homo aestheticus*.

---

[1] Abraham Kuyper, *Lectures on Calvinism* (Grand Rapids, MI: Eerdmans, 1931), 157 (paraphrased).
[2] Alexander Baumgarten first used "aesthetics" for the modern discipline in his dissertation "Philosophical Reflections on Some Matters Pertaining to Poetry."

## SOME DISTINCTIONS

Some distinguish between aesthetics, philosophy of art, and art criticism. In *aesthetics* we wonder about the nature of aesthetic objects (natural or human), the kinds of experiences associated with those objects, their beauty or ugliness, the content of aesthetic standards, if any, and the relation of aesthetics proper to philosophy of art. *Philosophy of art*, which is actually our main concern here, asks questions about artistic experience, the medium, technique, form, and subject matter of art, various artistic theories (such as imitation), the relation of symbol, truth, and morality to art, and how to interpret and judge it. *Art criticism* presupposes some background in aesthetics and philosophy of art. It is concerned with the analysis and evaluation of particular works of art for enhanced understanding and appreciation, say Beethoven's *Ninth*. For some, however, aesthetics in general, is superfluous: "Aesthetics is for art as ornithology is for the birds," said American artist Barnett Newman rather scathingly.[3]

## PLATO ON ART

Plato was leery about the arts for metaphysical and anthropological reasons. Since he believed ultimate reality resides in the upper world of the forms, focusing on artistic objects in the world below places observers three steps away from reality. Not only might mimetic artists know nothing about the things they depict, but also their images are a kind of metaphysical "cheat" as an imitation of an imitation that deceives and thwarts contemplation of heavenly realities.[4] Art, in other words, generates metaphysical illusions.

Art also had anthropological consequences. Plato feared the power of the arts to deform the rational character of decent people.

---

[3] Quoted in Arthur C. Danto, *The Abuse of Beauty: Aesthetics and the Concept of Art* (Peru, IL: Open Court, 2003), 1.

[4] See Plato's *Republic*, bk. 10, and the commentary on it by Dorothy L. Sayers, "Toward a Christian Esthetic," in *The Whimsical Christian: 18 Essays—Reflections on God and Man* (New York: Collier, 1978), 78.

The arts, he believed, stimulate the lowest part of the human soul and foster corybantic behaviors. They bar reason from governing people. In turn, artistically malformed people could undermine the judicious character of the state, which is, actually, a point worth pondering. In Plato's mind, therefore, art is guilty of two offenses: it is both deceptive and reason destroying.[5] Wordsmiths such as poets and rhetoricians were Plato's greatest concern. If their language was used maliciously, it could create indelible impressions of falsehood—inscriptions that corrupt the soul.

Regardless, Plato recognized the nuclear power of the arts and raised enduring questions about their value and purpose, and even the possible need for censorship. His reflections in this area clue us in that a key to changing a culture is to be found in changing its art. The worse the songs, stories, and so on, the worse off the world. The better the songs, stories, and so on, the better off the world. "Let me write the songs of a nation," someone has wisely noted, "and I care not who makes its laws."[6] Perhaps Christian philosophers should become artists, or at least add aesthetic dimensions to their philosophic work.

Given, then, the power of the arts, what does canonical Trinitarian theism contribute to a Christian aesthetic and philosophy of art? Though Dorothy Sayers was conflicted over the church's stance on art and uncertain about the existence of a Christian aesthetic, there has been considerable reflection and action on this topic over the years.[7]

## BEAUTY

Once upon a time, beauty was the sine qua non of the arts. Beautiful things elicit powerful responses, presumably aesthetic in

---

[5] Plato, *Republic*, trans. G. M. A. Grube, rev. C. D. C. Reeve, in *Plato: Complete Works*, ed. John M. Cooper and D. S. Hutchinson (Indianapolis: Hackett, 1997), 1209–10.

[6] This is attributed to many, Plato included.

[7] As a believer, Sayers claimed, "We have no Christian esthetic—no Christian philosophy of the arts. The Church as a body has never made up her mind about the arts, and it is hardly too much to say that she has never tried." See her "Toward a Christian Esthetic," 74.

nature. As Hans Urs von Balthasar has written, "Before the beautiful—no, not really *before* but *within* the beautiful—the whole person quivers. He not only 'finds' the beautiful moving; rather, he experiences himself as being moved and possessed by it."[8]

Recently, however, artists have been seeking to depict the uglier sides of life. In many contexts today, if a work of art does not display ugliness, albeit in a beautiful way, it's not art. In fact, if something is beautiful, it may be disregarded as mere sentimentality, and some of it, in fact, is. As a result, "beauticians," so to speak, have been put on the defensive and pressed into service as apologists for beauty. To vote for beauty is a minority position in various art worlds. Nonetheless, we need beautiful things, for things of beauty produce joy and help "tear off a little corner of the darkness," to borrow a Bono phrase.

Even if the notion of beauty is contested in certain circles, one thing the Christian vision is clear about is the beauty of God himself and that he is the source of all beauty. One of King David's deepest desires was to "gaze upon *the beauty of the* LORD and to inquire in his temple" (Ps. 27:4). On a similar note, Jonathan Edwards (1703–1758) waxed eloquent about God's beauty and attributed all beauty to him:

> For as God is infinitely the greatest being, so he is allowed to be infinitely the most beautiful and excellent: and all the beauty found throughout the whole creation, is but the reflection of the diffused beams of that Being who hath an infinite fullness of brightness and glory . . . . [he is] the foundation and fount of all being and all beauty; . . . much more than the sun is the fountain and summary comprehension of all the light and brightness of the day.[9]

---

[8] Hans Urs von Balthasar, *Seeing the Form*, trans. Erasmo Leiva-Merikakis, vol. 1 of *The Glory of the Lord: A Theological Aesthetics*, ed. Joseph Fessio, SJ, and John Riches (San Francisco: Ignatius Press, 1982), 247 (emphasis original).

[9] Jonathan Edwards, *The Nature of True Virtue* (Ann Arbor, MI: Ann Arbor Paperbacks, 1960), 14–15.

I can't help but think that God's own beauty makes beauty itself objective. This would be similar to the way his righteous constitution grounds objective morality. In other words, beauty is not purely subjective in the eye of the beholder. Rather, it is really and truly there in God in a transcendent way. There are aesthetic red lights and aesthetic green lights in the universe. Certainly cultural and personal factors influence our expression, apprehension, and appreciation of beauty. The aesthetically subjective enters in at these and perhaps other levels.

Of course, we don't have ten aesthetic or artistic commandments like we have the ten moral commandments. Apparently, the infinitely beautiful God has left it up to us in our cultural undertakings to discern the character of true beauty. What have we come up with in our investigations? Theologically informed Christian thinkers have seized upon the notions of unity, proportion, harmony, order, brightness, clarity, color, and pleasure to describe, if not define, the beautiful as such. Apprehension of beauty may also be intuitive. Don't we perceive the balanced as beautiful? Augustine thought so, and he believed we should trace these aesthetic sensitivities back to God himself. Here's his example:

> And so I [Augustine] inquire of an architect, who has just built one arch, why he is at pains to make the one on the other side its exact equivalent, he will answer, I believe, that it is to have the parts of the building corresponding in every way to their opposite numbers. And if I press on with my questioning and ask why he is making that choice, he will say that this is how it should be, that this is beautiful, that this is what pleases the eye of the beholder. . . . [But he] does not understand what he is depending on for his answer [viz., God].[10]

The beauty, then, we detect easily in creation is rooted in and

---

[10] Augustine, *True Religion* (*De vera religione*), trans. Edmund Hill, OP, part 1, vol. 8, *On Christian Belief, The Works of Saint Augustine: A Translation for the 21st Century*, ed. John E. Rotelle and Boniface Ramsey (Hyde Park, NY: New City Press, 2005), 69.

a reflection of God's beauty. Beauty is his workmanship, as even an indolent observer driving along the Pacific Coast Highway in northern California in the Big Sur region should be able to see. Creation's beauty should lead us back to creation's God, if we have eyes and ears to see and hear, or a heart that makes such seeing and hearing possible.

Not only is beauty a God thing, but human artistic expression itself may be a vestige of the Trinity, as Dorothy Sayers believes. She thinks that the idea, energy, and power of a work of art correspond to the eternal nature of the Father, Son, and Holy Spirit. Like the persons of God the Trinity, these three features of an artwork are distinguishable and yet undivided.[11] Human artistic endeavors, then, not only reflect God's beauty but may be a mark of the mystery of the Trinity. To be sure, beauty and the arts are the gifts of God, and though spoiled by sin, they are yet redeemed in Christ.

## A BIBLICAL FRAMEWORK

We can affirm biblically that our creative artistic aspirations and contributions have a divine source. On the basis of the creation stories in Genesis 1–2, one of the traits God has shared with us as his image and likeness is craftsmanship in the richest sense of this word. Bezalel, whom God called to ply his trades in constructing the tabernacle, is a good example (Exodus 31).

There is one caveat, however. God's creative handiwork was out of nothing (*ex nihilo*), whereas ours is derived from divinely made, preexisting raw materials (*creatio*, i.e., *ex creatio*). Our art, even our philosophy, is always on God's dime, so to speak (like a child's gift for a parent that's funded by the parent). Our creative activity is best understood analogously, then, to be like God's and yet quite different.

Unfortunately, sin has severely defaced us as God's image and as artists. It has darkened our minds, perverted our wills, and put

---

[11] Dorothy L. Sayers, *The Mind of the Maker* (1941; repr. San Francisco: Harper & Row, 1979), chap. 3.

God's very good creation into eclipse. Our ignorance is pervasive. Our desires have gone haywire. We are bent and broken, and our art follows suit. Can a ready-made object, like a urinal, really be great art? What about crucifixes immersed in beakers of urine? Is slicing one's self with a razor blade in a performance piece to be admired? Art, in other words, frequently conveys the depravity of the human artists who make it.

These considerations raise important questions. Can art be redeemed? Does Jesus's work of salvation have aesthetic implications? Undoubtedly! Jesus's work of salvation is comprehensive in scope and encompasses the arts. Indeed, his death and resurrection entail all cultural enterprises, as his grace restores nature—and, yes, art.

To begin with, Jesus's incarnation discloses the goodness of the material world and the value of human creatureliness. It also implies that creation and human existence are worthy of careful study and artistic expression. Christ's incarnation certifies an artist's immersion in cultural and artistic pursuits. Artistic expression itself may also be a kind of mini-incarnation as our thoughts, feelings, and ideas show up in wood, metal, clay, sounds, words, dance moves, algorithms, and so on.

Art, then, is creationally affirmed and redeemed in Jesus Christ. Insofar as believing artists claim this big biblical story as their own, their overall bodies of their work ought to convey its fundamental plot sequence. This would include the *wonders* of creation, the *heartbreak* of sin, and the *hope* of redemption. That is, believing artists should communicate the way things are supposed to be (creation), the way they actually are (fallen), and the way they can be already, and one day shall fully be (redeemed).[12]

In defense of beauty (or at least assuming its identification with the artistic), Abraham Kuyper thought that in light of canonical Christian theism, art ought to help us recall the beauties of the

---

unspoiled creation that are now lost and to foresee the even greater glories of the world to come:

> But if you confess that the world once *was* beautiful, but by the curse has become *undone*, and by a final catastrophe is to pass to its full state of glory, excelling even the beautiful of paradise, then art has the mystical task of reminding us in its productions of the beautiful that was lost and of anticipating its perfect coming luster.[13]

## DANCE AND FILM

The Bible is not a textbook on aesthetics, philosophy of art, art criticism, or any other cultural enterprise, such as philosophy, for that matter. It's not the *Encyclopedia Britannica*. Rather, the Bible's particular purpose is doxological and soteriological, having been written to glorify God in telling the redemption story through Israel, Christ, and the church. Despite its restricted purpose, the Scriptures do speak *to* most everything, including various arts such as literature, poetry, music, and drama. It gives us a framework for considering various fields of endeavor like these. I have found the Scripture's insights on *dancing* to be particularly informative, especially in light of Christian suspicions over this particular "Hebraic" art form.

Dance is structurally good, yet it does go off the tracks. Contemporary examples abound of what we might call *dirty dancing*. These might be like the type of dancing associated with the worship of the golden calf in Exodus 32:19 and Salome's dance that led to the beheading of John the Baptist (Matt. 14:6; Mark 6:22). These, and others, are suggestive of the dangers born of *misdirected* forms of dancing that have given this art form a bad name. We don't, however, want to reject the essential along with the inessential.

At the opposite end of the spectrum, of course, is *sacred*

---

[13] Kuyper, *Lectures*, 155.

*dancing.* Whirling about was taken for granted as a natural part of worship in ancient Israel. Miriam and the women celebrated the exodus with dancing (Ex. 15:20–21). David danced before the Lord with all his might when the ark was returned to Jerusalem (2 Sam. 6:12–19). God is to be praised, say Psalm 149:3 and Psalm 150:4, with dancing.

As Stewart Headlam has suggested, sacred dance is an outward and visible sign of an inward and spiritual grace. In defense of a sacramental perspective on the world, he said, "Your Manichaean Protestant and your superfine rationalist, rejects the dance as worldly, frivolous, sensual, and so forth; and your dull, stupid sensualist sees legs, and grunts with some satisfaction: but your sacramentalist knows something worth more than both of these. He knows . . . that the poetry of dance is the expression of unseen spiritual grace."[14]

Finally, the Bible also authorizes dancing as a celebration of life and of life's events. Sad times should elicit mourning and tears. Good times should prompt laughter and dancing. There is a providentially ordered season and a time for every matter under heaven, including "a time to mourn, and a time to dance" (Eccles. 3:4). God can even turn the former into the latter (Ps. 30:11). Jesus himself said that the homecoming of the prodigal was celebrated with music and dancing (Luke 15:25). Jesus is Lord of the dance!

> Dance, then, wherever you may be;
> I am the Lord of the Dance said He;
> And I'll lead you all wherever you may be
> and I'll lead you all in the Dance said He![15]

In addition to its physiological aspect, dance also evokes deep emotions. So does film. Of course, we lack explicit biblical input

---

[14] Stewart Headlam, quoted in Frank Kermode, *What Is Dance? Readings in Theory and Criticism,* ed. Roger Copeland and Marshall Cohen (New York: Oxford University Press, 1983), 141.
[15] The song "Lord of the Dance" was written by Sydney Carter (1915–2004), http://www.stainer.co.uk/lotd.html.

on film, but we do have an anthropology derived from Scripture that can deepen our film theories. If human beings as God's image are embodied, communal, narratively based creatures of love, affection, and desire, then what implications might this sort of human identity have on both movie making and movie viewing? In other words, a holistic view of human persons as God's image has holistic consequences when it comes to movies.

For one thing, films affect us physically regardless of genre—action, adventure, comedy, tragedy, horror, romance, and so on. "When we watch a film," as Torben Grodal states, "our heart rhythms change, we sweat, and our muscles alternately tense and relax throughout."[16] For another, films affect us emotionally. Carl Plantinga, for example, challenges theories that reduce movies to messages since we are more than just cognitive beings. In Plantinga's question, "Are all of these affective elements of film spectatorship mere epiphenomena, the throwaway detritus of what is worthwhile about the film viewing experience?"[17] Unlikely, though those who remain under a residual Cartesian paradigm might tend to think so.

Hence, the aesthetics of movie making and movie viewing, under the influence of a solid Christian anthropology, should be all-inclusive in nature—entailing the physiological, the emotional or affective, the mental, and so on. Our bodies, hearts, and minds with all their intricately connected faculties, must be taken into cinematic consideration.

## SOME VIEWPOINTS ON ART

Some theologically informed perspectives will help round out our reflections on a Christian aesthetics and philosophy of art. First, *art is for the glory of God*. God's own handiwork declares his glory, and so should ours. Our singing, playing, painting, writing,

---

[16] Torben Grodal, *Embodied Visions: Evolution, Emotion, Culture and Film* (New York: Oxford University Press, 2009), 4.
[17] Carl Plantinga, *Moving Viewers: American Film and the Spectator's Experience* (Berkeley, CA: University of California Press, 2009), 3.

and so forth should speak not only well of us but also of God, who gave us the ability to make the art in the first place. It should honor him in meaningful ways, as our creativity and cleverness display his own. We learn to admire and respect the Creator through the imaginative works of the creature. As Paul says in a concluding doxology in Romans 11:36, "For from him and through him and to him are all things. To him be glory forever. Amen."

Second, *art fulfills the artist.* I imagine that God's original work of creation and his work of new creation brought a sense of joy to his heart. Likewise, we are most fulfilled when we make something new as well. Though satisfaction comes in many forms, to make or create in an imaginative way has to be one of the most satisfying activities in which we can participate. How gratifying is a project well done, whether painting a picture, composing a song, writing a poem, mowing the lawn, writing a paper, or completing a book!

Third, *art reduces anxiety.* If we are worried about food, consider the birds of the air. They neither sow, nor reap, nor gather into barns, and yet God feeds them, and we are of greater value than the birds. If we are anxious about clothing, then we should consider the lilies. God clothes the fields with these nonlaboring flowers in ways that even exceed Solomon's attire. God providentially cares for the birds and the blooms, and this shows us we need not worry about anything. Artists of all kinds observe and depict God's provision inside and out and help us to trust in his provision. Artistry under God, in other words, tranquilizes and frees us up to seek God's kingdom first in all things.[18]

Fourth, *art blesses others.* Art is not purely autotelic, certainly not in the bohemian sense of art for art's sake (*l'art pour l'art*). Like the food we enjoy yet with an energizing purpose, so also it is with art. It is inherently good, yet it also blesses by immersing us in beauty by poignantly calling our numbed attention to overlooked

---

[18] Makoto Fujimura, "Artist's Introduction," *The Four Holy Gospels* (Wheaton: Crossway, 2010), *ix.*

things and by challenging our hackneyed modes of thought and ways of life. Art, in short, edifies.

Finally, *common grace enables believers to appreciate the artistic contributions of non-Christians.* There is considerable artistic "Egyptian gold" to relish, even if it is produced by those who reject Christ. There are also some moral limits on what we can enjoy as well. We need Spirit-led discernment to select what is best to engage or disengage. All things are lawful, but not all things are profitable (1 Cor. 6:12).

In any case, here are two rules of thumb to follow. First, we shouldn't try to justify fallen artistic expressions or aesthetic participation on the basis of God's good creation. At the same time we should not reject artistic expressions or participation outright because of the world. We need deep spiritual insight on what to accept on the basis of common grace and what to reject in light of the antithesis. Second, we should commit, as Paul instructs in Romans 14:13, never to "pass judgment on one another any longer, but rather decide never to put a stumbling block or hindrance in the way of a brother." In the end, no work of art is more important than the Christian life, and we need to support each other in weaving together a fabric of Christian faithfulness. For, indeed, the Christian life itself ought to be a thing of truth, goodness, and beauty in the midst of a mendacious, evil, and ugly world.[19] Believers are God's workmanship, literally his *poiema*, his poem (Eph. 2:20).

## CONCLUSION: ARTISTIC KNOWLEDGE AND INSPIRATION

How might an aesthetics and philosophy of art in the framework of Christian faith be instructive on its own and generate creative, critical, and complementary engagement with aesthetics and philosophy of art in general? What do Christian and non-Christian

---

[19] Francis A. Schaeffer, *Art and the Bible: Two Essays* (Downers Grove, IL: InterVarsity, 1973), 94. Schaeffer offers eleven total perspectives on art from the vantage point of Christian conviction.

thinkers have in common on various artistic and aesthetic matters? Over what might they agree or disagree? How might a Christian philosophy of the arts provide constructive criticism of the work of aestheticians and philosophers of art who have little or no room for Christian ideas in their reflections? Where and how might Christian thought fill in the blanks in this realm of consideration and offer a more complete picture? How might philosophic insights, in turn, critically assist Christian reflection and stimulate fresh Christian thinking in aesthetics and philosophy of art?

For example, I have been stimulated to think more deeply about the nature of poetic knowledge and artistic inspiration by Plato's dialogue *Ion*.[20] Is Ion the rhapsodist able to speak the truth and move an audience because of his knowledge? Or is it because he is inspired? If poets are inspired, are they, then, out of their minds or even under demonic control when they compose, given the Platonic doctrine of inspiration? Do rhapsodists like Ion recite a poet's work in this same frenzied condition? Plato indicates that poetic inspiration was a form of madness that came from the gods and was passed along to an audience through a speaker. The irrational effects of inspired poetic composition and recitation have a detrimental impact on the people who listen to it. At the same time, a Christian aesthetic philosophy would offer an alternative understanding of poetic inspiration combining pneumatology and common grace and placing moral and spiritual responsibility upon an audience for its reactions to portrayed events.

A Christian-based aesthetic and philosophy of the arts and regular philosophic reflection over traditional and contemporary theories of art and aesthetic experience, as well as perspectives on individual arts including literature, drama, painting, architecture, film, music, and dance ought to be equally stimulating and mutually fruitful.

---

[20] Plato, *Ion*, trans. Paul Woodruff, in *Plato: Complete Works*, ed. John M. Cooper and D. S. Hutchinson (Indianapolis: Hackett, 1997), 937–49.

# ✚ 7

# THE VOCATION OF CHRISTIAN PHILOSOPHERS

He who marries the spirit of the age will soon become a widower.
—Dean William R. Inge

Philosophers ask questions and think about things that most people take for granted, such as the nature of the vocations of Christian philosophers. Few Christian philosophers even think about this one. We pretty much follow the patterns set by Socrates, Plato, Aristotle, or whomever, in doing our philosophic work. Or we may embrace current trends in the academy or in the various academic guilds. Or we might combine these two sets of influences in some creative way. However, Jesus Christ has set the example for Christian philosophers. Here's a question, then, for us to consider: Is Jesus Christ Lord of our philosophical callings?

Why do I pursue this inquiry? Because it seems to me that a fair number of those who claim to be Christian philosophers assume various stances associated with this discipline that are unbecoming of followers of Christ. I'm sure I'm among their number. This situation is a proverbial "elephant in the room" and has been ignored long enough. Whether Christian philosophers are thinking, teaching, and living in a manner worthy of the gospel is a matter that ought to be addressed. We Christian philosophers are in need of some advice that will enable us to ply our trade in a manner more pleasing to the Lord.

## PLATO'S CONCERNS

Obviously, Plato wasn't concerned about Christians in philosophy. Nonetheless, he was concerned about the impact of philosophy on young thinkers even at thirty years of age. He believed a connection between philosophers and philosophy could truly be a dangerous liaison, if precautions weren't taken along the way.[1] The undesirable traits that Plato feared philosophy could impart to its practitioners have shown up among Christian philosophers as well—young and old alike. Plato's concerns are thus our concerns, and we can learn from him what to watch out for in our own encounter with philosophy. Here are three things that concerned Plato.

First, he worried that those who were introduced to philosophy might no longer honor the convictions they received from their families earlier on in their lives. In a similar way, I have seen the Christian beliefs of young Christian philosophers demoted to a secondary status, if not forsaken altogether, as they are exposed to "higher-level thinking." Plato told a story to convey his point. He said that if a young person should discover his alleged parents were really not his parents, he would no longer honor them. Similarly, if a young philosopher, in the absence of truth, discovers new ideas and ways of life that flatter him, he probably would not continue to honor what he was taught early on in life. In the process, young philosophers reject their patrimonial beliefs and ways of life.[2] Furthermore, in the midst of this transition, the demeanor of these individuals changes, as they tend to become more unruly than upright. They swing from a more restrained lifestyle to liberality.

To be sure, it's good for young people to examine things carefully and to make needed changes. However, in the midst of the

[1] Plato, *Republic*, trans. G. M. A. Grube, rev. C. D. C. Reeve, in *Plato: Complete Works*, ed. John M. Cooper and D. S. Hutchinson (Indianapolis: Hackett, 1997), 1151–55.
[2] Ibid., 1153.

examination and change, they should cleave to that which is still good (1 Thess. 5:21). They don't need to throw out the baby with the bathwater.

Second, Plato was concerned that if young philosophers are exposed to "dialectic" or "arguments," they might misuse their newly acquired philosophical powers to argue with others and refute them purely for argument's sake. For Plato, the problem wasn't lodged in philosophical knowledge or skills per se, but in their use merely to win arguments. It's natural, of course, to want to employ a newly acquired body of knowledge and skill set, but these things need to be employed for the right reasons, namely, to become wise and live well.

This other dishonorable approach we copy from our mentors. We've seen our teachers use philosophy to skewer an opponent. We will follow suit, maybe even as a show-off, as it were. Plato knew that we are natural born imitators, especially of those we admire. If we observed our mentors engaging in triumphal dialectic, we will do the same. We would simply be imitating the teachers whom we look up to, but for less than noble ends.[3]

Third, Plato feared the possibility of skepticism. Since young "puppies" have experienced both victory and defeat in dialectic, they learn rather quickly that no ideas can stand the test of rigorous examination. There are always defeaters for arguments. There are also defeaters for these defeaters. There are, additionally, defeaters for the defeaters of defeaters. Is nothing, then, nailed down, we might wonder? We find ourselves emulating this certain uncertainty as skepticism lurks around the corner.

If this is the consequence of philosophy, Plato wondered whether even thirty-year-olds should get a taste for arguments. If Plato was concerned about thinkers at this age, shouldn't we be as concerned about introducing philosophy to *Christian* students in their late teens or early twenties?

---

[3] Ibid., 1154.

In any case, Plato himself believed that great caution must be exercised when introducing younger people to philosophy. For him, nothing less than the credibility of the philosophical way of life was at stake. It was supposed to make people wise—lovers of truth and wisdom. Instead, it seems it can cause young pups to forsake their former convictions and turn them into arrogant, intellectual brats. As miscreants, they could potentially discredit the entire philosophic way.

Plato was certain that more mature thinkers would not fall into such traps. Instead, they would use their intellectual gifts for the honorable purpose of searching for truth, and students would copy these teachers who modeled this kind of integrity for them. Together, they would lend prestige to the philosophical enterprise, since it has proven to make people wiser and more virtuous.[4]

Obviously, the notion of imitation was at the heart of Plato's philosophy of education, an important point worth pondering for its contemporary implications and applications. We learn what we live (or what is lived before us). Unfortunately, some philosophers have fostered infidelity, rowdiness, conceit, and skepticism in their younger charges by example. While fostering resistance to the "system" can be healthy, the need for care remains. We don't want to produce budding young nihilists, do we? Perhaps the Old Testament prophets, Jesus the Messiah, and the New Testament apostles are good examples of proper forms of opposition.

Jacques Maritain was an outstanding example of a godly philosopher worthy of imitation for a younger Ralph McInerny. McInerny paid the French Thomist the highest possible compliment in recalling the last lecture he gave at the Moreau Seminary on the Notre Dame campus on an autumn night in 1958. Of Maritain the man and the impact the evening had on him, McInerny said:

---

[4] Ibid.

He was a saintly man. That is what I sensed as I scuffled through the leaves on my way back from Maritain's last lecture at Moreau. . . . He loved the truth but his purpose in life was not to win arguments. He wanted to be wise. Such an odd ambition for a philosopher! He succeeded because he prayed as well as he studied.[5]

Experiences like this one may be one of the best reasons for going to college or university, especially a Christian one in the area of philosophy. Let us, then, be imitators of our teachers and professors as they are of Christ (1 Cor. 11:1).

## PHILOSOPHIES OF THE PHILOSOPHIC VOCATION

Plato was concerned about the way philosophy might impact its people. Plato's Socrates is at the head of the pack, as we shall see below. Meanwhile, we can take a look at how leading thinkers and schools of thought in the history of philosophy have established precedents for what it means to be philosophers and to practice the discipline. Meanwhile, we ask: To whom have you hitched your philosophical wagon? To what school of thought do you adhere? Is Jesus Lord of your philosophical calling?

A survey of some leading philosophies of philosophy shows us that there are some things, whether stylistically or substantively, that Christian faith would admonish us to shun or embrace in philosophy. What can we follow? What should we reject? Where does common grace set in? Where does the antithesis come into play? The point is this: Christian philosophers should do their best to imitate Christ, not Socrates, Plato, Aristotle, or whomever, in their philosophical vocations.

Postmodernism's collapse into indeterminacy is a significant weakness, yet its recognition of the implications of narratives, communities, embodiment, history, race, sex, and class make

---

[5] Ralph McInerny, *Notre Dame Magazine* (Summer 1985), quoted in James V. Schall, *Another Sort of Learning: Selected Contrary Essays* (San Francisco: Ignatius, 1988), 48.

aspects of it attractive. We resist modernism's arch-rationalism as dehumanizing and its thoroughgoing scientism as reductionistic, and yet we recognize the value of its contributions. Though difficult to describe, the emphasis of Continental thought on phenomenology, embodiment, gender, tradition, history, power, and the existential are generally laudable. Yet the Continental devaluation of logic and its self-defeating rejection of metanarratives are drawbacks. Analytic philosophy focuses on the importance of linguistic clarity and logical cogency, yet this strength can become a weakness if it reduces the whole of philosophy to technicalities. Analytic philosophy can become inapt, dry, and tedious in its obsession with logic chopping. Do Christian philosophers really want to invest their lives, teaching, and influence in fostering disciples to this approach to philosophy? To be sure, facets of these philosophical traditions are worthy of emulation by Christian thinkers, but some are jejune. What ever happened to the idea that philosophy is supposed to be the love of wisdom?

To continue, the Thomistic recognition of revelation and its harmony with reason are pluses, but insofar as it apparently endows human thought with a significant measure of pretended autonomy causes us to wonder. Does grace perfect nature, as the Thomist tradition seems to advocate?[6]

I have hitched my philosophical wagon to Augustine because he does philosophy in a prayerful way before the face of God (coram Deo). He also believed that grace restores nature and Christ converts philosophy. Also, his idea of faith seeking understanding (of itself and everything else) is for me the sine qua non of Christian philosophy. On the other hand, Augustine's residual neo-Platonism can be a source of grief as well.

Aristotle's fearlessness in divinizing his metaphysics, the power of his insights, his helpful distinctions, and the sheer breadth of

---

[6] An example is John Paul II, *Fides et Ratio*, Encyclical Letter to the Bishops of the Catholic Church on the Relationship of Faith and Reason, Vatican translation (Boston: Pauline Books & Media, 1998), 18–19.

his philosophic inquiries are appealing. I have learned much from him, even if he can be somewhat dry.

Of course, Plato's Socrates has been a primary philosophical pacesetter. Many get an image of what a philosopher is and does from him. The sources of our knowledge about Socrates are a bit uncertain, yet some things are clear.[7] Socrates considered himself to be an intellectual "midwife." He helped others give birth to truth out of their own minds and lives. He exercised his midwifery through rigorous conversation or *dialectic*, through question and answer, and by presenting and refuting arguments. Socrates interrogatively challenged the ideas of the people he spoke with as most philosophers do. Talking and arguing back and forth were the key components of his method. Socrates spent his days in great conversations out of which he believed truth would bubble up.

Furthermore, Socrates was modest enough to be proven wrong, and he was courageous enough to show others the error of their ways. He was happy to do the latter, even happier if the former occurred. If they didn't challenge each other, how else could he or others become better? For Socrates, knowledge was the key to life, especially self-knowledge. People were his passion. He sought to know himself and encouraged others to do the same. The most important thing we could do is examine our lives— "The unexamined life is not worth living"[8]—and seek, according to the Delphic Oracle, to know oneself. In all these things, we can follow suit.

Other facets of Socrates's life and teachings as a philosopher raise questions. His self-proclaimed agnosticism and his flirtations with the skeptics are perhaps the most egregious. His excessive rationalism is at times repelling. He could also be rather priggish, smug, rude, and exasperating, traits unbecoming of Christian philosophers.

---

[7] This summary of Socrates is based on *Symposium* 223d; *Memorabilia* 1.3.5; *Theatetus* 150c-d; *Meno* 86b-c; *Gorgias* 458a; 460b; *Apology* 38a.
[8] *Apology* 38a.

Plato's description of Thales of Miletus has also been influential in establishing a pattern for philosophers to follow. In his dialogue *Theaetetus*, Plato presents Thales as an otherworldly, impractical, and virtually disembodied human being who remains "blissfully" unaware of the ordinary affairs of daily life (e.g., the locations of public assemblies, political laws and life, social customs). In the *Theaetetus*, for example, Socrates's conversation partner Theodorus asks Socrates about the meaning of Thales's philosophic disregard for worldly affairs. Socrates responds with a humorous story about a young Thracian girl who ridicules him for falling into a well as he contemplated the heavens. He failed to see what is right in front of him.[9] Thales's philosophical model stands in jarring contrast to the example of Christ incarnate, who integrated heaven and earth, was pragmatic in his teachings, and was fully human in both body and soul. Christian philosophers would do well to reject the former example and embrace the latter, even though Thales's model reigns.

Alvin Plantinga has recognized how easy it is to be a philosophical chameleon. We typically fall in lockstep with those around us. "Philosophy is a social enterprise;" he writes, "and our standards and assumptions—the parameters within which we practice our craft—are set by our mentors and by the great contemporary centers of philosophy."[10] However, and this is a big *however*, Plantinga's primary point, and mine, is to say that Christian philosophers shouldn't be too quick to embrace historic or contemporary philosophic fashions and ideas unless they fit well with our Christian commitments. Christian philosophers, in other words, should get their marching orders from God, Scripture, and the church. Our teaching, research, and service in church and at the academy ought to prove it.

---

[9] Plato, *Theaetetus*, trans. M. J. Levett, rev. Myles Burnyeat, in *Plato: Complete Works*, ed. John M. Cooper and D. S. Hutchinson (Indianapolis: Hackett, 1997), 193.

[10] Alvin Plantinga, "Advice to Christian Philosophers," *Faith and Philosophy* 1 (1984): 255.

## MAX WEBER'S VISION OF THE ACADEMIC VOCATION

The famous German sociologist and political economist Max Weber delivered an influential lecture at Munich University in 1918 titled "*Wissenschaft als Beruf*," or "Science [or Academics] as Vocation."[11] Its influence traversed the Atlantic and has shaped the American understanding of the academic vocation especially in research contexts. Along with many others in the American academy, Christian philosophers have adjusted themselves comfortably to Weber's vision of their scholarly callings.

Weber situates academic vocation in the context of naturalism in metaphysics, rationalism in epistemology, and scientism in methodology. Weber disenchanted the world. He was committed to these beliefs as his Weltanschauung. He was consistent in spelling out an objective and factual model of the academic vocation in accordance with his premises. "The task of the teacher," he stated, "is to serve the students with his knowledge and scientific experience and not to imprint upon them his personal political [or religious] views."[12]

Failing to recognize this, and craving moral leadership from their professors, students listen to lectures, hoping for something more than "just the facts." The problem, Weber said, is that such students misunderstand the nature of the academic vocation. They will be disappointed if they expect more from their professors than the academic and scientific, for they are to be academics and scientists and these things *alone*. This may be something for which we might be thankful. Still, this would include a potential disappointment in philosophy faculty who are supposed to be lovers of wisdom. Many are mere technicians or even possibly anarchists.

Alvin Plantinga's "Advice to Christian Philosophers" and

---

[11] Max Weber, "Science as Vocation," in *From Max Weber: Essays in Sociology*, trans. and ed. H. H. Gerth and C. Wright Mills (New York: Oxford University Press, 1946), 129–56.
[12] Ibid., 146.

Nicholas Wolterstorff's *Reason within the Bounds of Religion* offer steps to help remedy this problem. Plantinga has advised Christian academics—philosophers in particular—to take certain biblical doctrines as assumptions in their philosophic work. Similarly, Wolterstorff has argued that the religious commitments of Christian scholars, including philosophers, ought to function as "control beliefs" in their devising and weighing of theories.[13]

Plantinga's and Wolterstorff's recommendations are courageous and radical when compared to the ways in which the philosophic community secularly socializes and even seduces its devotees. In addition to this cognitive aspect, however, more is needed. The substance, friendships, liturgies, and encouragement of Christian communities are also necessary in nurturing Christian philosophers who are seeking to fulfill their academic vocations in faithful ways according to the will of God. As philosophic communities shape their adherents in one direction, churches and Christian communities ought to be resources of a uniquely Christian counter-formation with academic implications such as the following.

## TRAITS OF CHRISTIAN PHILOSOPHERS

On the basis of Christ's incarnation, life and ministry, crucifixion, resurrection, ascension, cosmic authority, gift of the Holy Spirit, and coming judgment we are able to identify eight Christlike traits of Christian philosophy, Christian philosophers, and the Christian philosophical vocation. First, since the eternal Son of God and the second person of the Trinity became flesh and dwelt among us, we have to rethink the nature, content, and practice of philosophy. The earthly visitation of ultimate reality and true being in the person and work of Jesus Christ changes everything—philosophy included.

Dietrich Bonhoeffer recognized the implications of Jesus's

---

[13] Alvin Plantinga, "Advice to Christian Philosophers," 253–71; and Nicholas Wolterstorff, *Reason within the Bounds of Religion*, 2nd ed. (Grand Rapids, MI: Eerdmans, 1984), chaps. 1, 10, and 11.

coming on the discipline of philosophy and promulgated the "Christological Redescription of Philosophy" as a result.[14] For Bonhoeffer, Christian philosophy (*christliche Philosophie*) was "a kind of theological thinking which is grounded in the primacy of revelation and shaped by receptivity to otherness."[15] To employ the more concrete terms we have been using in this book, philosophy has to be rethought in light of canonical Trinitarian theism.

Second, the Christian philosophical vocation is characterized by service for others. This can take many forms including reading, research, writing, publication, public witness, teaching, mentoring, and collegiality. In his own life and ministry, Jesus was "the man for others," to use a Bonhoefferism once again. Christian philosophers should be Christian philosophers for others. This will undermine the self-service and self-promotion that so often constitute the aspirations of professional philosophers.

Third, the Christian philosophical vocation is cruciform in nature. A calling to philosophy in Christ not only means serving others but also entails suffering and sacrifice on their behalf. Christians are to deny themselves, take up their cross, and follow Jesus (Matt. 16:24; Mark 8:34; Luke 9:23). No less is required of Christian philosophers.

What might cruciform philosophy or cruciform philosophers look like? It probably means disciplined work and rigorous study. It probably means taking a stand for truth, goodness or morality, and beauty. It probably means being a public disciple of Jesus. It probably means doing philosophy on behalf of the church. It probably means choosing neglected research topics of concern to Christian communities. It probably means basing philosophical work on countercultural Christian assumptions. It probably means

---

[14] Charles Marsh, *Reclaiming Bonhoeffer: The Promise of His Theology* (New York: Oxford University Press, 1994), chap. 3. For Mark A. Noll, *Jesus Christ and the Life of the Mind* (Grand Rapids, MI: Eerdmans, 2011), Christ is the basis for the life of the Christian mind. Shouldn't he be for philosophy as well?

[15] Marsh, *Reclaiming Bonhoeffer*, 56.

a genuine concern for classroom excellence. It probably means loving and forgiving colleagues. It probably means genuine concern for students. It probably means studying theology in-depth. It may mean inglorious institutional affiliation. It surely means following a Jesus who "humbled himself by becoming obedient to the point of death, even death on a cross" (Phil. 2:8).

Fourth, the Christian philosophic vocation is enlivened with the power of Christ's resurrection. Sin turned the world into a cosmic cemetery, and some philosophers and philosophy departments exude that exact atmosphere. However, Christ trampled down death by his own death and defeated it thoroughly by his resurrection. His triumph inaugurated the kingdom of God and installed eternal life. Christian philosophers share in his victory. Fashionable philosophical pessimism, cynicism, and despair must give way to genuine faith, hope, and love born of Christ's conquest over all the malignant forces in the world. A genuine joy and power, shorn clean of sentimentalism, ought to characterize the life and labors of Christian philosophers.

Fifth, the Christian philosophic vocation is encased in the intercessory prayers of Christ. Jesus's ascension to God's right hand means many things theologically, but one of the most important is the role he assumed as advocate for his people. He ever lives to pray for the saints, including his thinkers. We need each others' prayers, to be sure, but it's encouraging and comforting to know that "we have an advocate with the Father, Jesus Christ the righteous" (1 John 2:1). Jesus was crucified, rose from the dead, abides at God's right hand, and now regularly intercedes on our behalf (Rom. 8:34; see also Heb. 7:25). Christian philosophers ought to be fortified by the fact that the ascended Christ supports their academic vocations in his prayers.

Sixth, the Christian philosophic vocation acknowledges and is subservient to the cosmic rule and authority of Christ. In ascending to the right hand of God, Christ assumed all authority in heaven and on earth (Matt. 28:18; Acts 2:34–36). Though there are many kings and many lords, Christ is King of kings and Lord of lords (Rev. 19:16). One day, at the name of Jesus every knee shall bow and every tongue will confess that Jesus Christ is Lord to the glory of God the Father (Phil. 2:11). Christian philosophers ought to recognize and submit to this reality now in all aspects of their lives and thought.

Seventh, the Christian philosophic vocation is endowed with the power of the Holy Spirit. Two central mistakes of the human race in all eras have been the radical quest for autonomy and an unfounded reliance on themselves. Of course, if we seek to live independently of God, we have nothing left to trust except ourselves and our own resources. This quest for self-sufficiency probably explains the rise of humanism, rationalism, empiricism, scientism, technologism, and economism in recent centuries.

On the other hand, Christ followers, including those of the philosophic clan, have been given the gifts of the guidance and strength, the comfort and courage, and the grace and truth born of the Holy Spirit. Christ promised upon his departure that he would not leave his disciples as orphans but would come to them in the person and work of the Spirit (John 14–16). He fulfilled this promise on the day of Pentecost (Acts 2). Ever since, the Spirit has been giving gifts to the body of Christ and fulfilling multiple promises, including the philosophically significant ones of helping disciples recall Christ's teachings and guiding them in regard to the truth. This pneumatological benefaction is certainly a blessing for Christian thinkers, and it should even give them a philosophical edge.

Eighth and finally, practitioners of a Christian philosophic vocation will one day be judged for their fidelity or infidelity to the way in which they conducted their callings as Christian philosophers. Summing up many biblical texts (e.g., 2 Cor. 5:10), the Nicene Creed states forthrightly that Jesus will come again "in glory to judge the living and the dead." Of course, those serious about honoring Christ in philosophy will desire sincerely to affirm the following along with Paul:

> I have fought the good fight, I have finished the race, I have kept the faith. Henceforth there is laid up for me the crown of righteousness, which the Lord, the righteous judge, will award to me on that Day. (2 Tim. 4:7–8a)

On this final exam day, you'll want to be able to hold your head up high and look him in the eye because you sang his song on the shores of Babylon.[16]

## CONCLUSION

With Christ at the center, philosophy itself becomes iridescent, and philosophers themselves become lovers. Etymologically, the term *philosophy* is a combination of the Greek words for love (*philia*) and wisdom (*sophia*). It means, of course, the "love of wisdom." However, as Augustine noted, not all who are philosophers are lovers of the true wisdom. God is the true wisdom. Therefore, a true philosopher is a lover of God.[17] In the end, this is what it means for Christian philosophers to affirm genuinely that Jesus Christ is Lord of philosophy.

---

[16] Inspired by Switchfoot, "Home Where I Belong," from the album *Vice Verses*, 2011.
[17] Quoted in Colin Brown, *Christianity and Western Thought: A History of Philosophers, Ideas and Movements*, vol. 1 of From the Ancient World to the Age of Enlightenment (Downers Grove, IL: InterVarsity, 1990), 98.

# QUESTIONS FOR REFLECTION

1) What is a philosophic prolegomena, and why is it important? Why might some omit this initial step in their philosophizing? What is your prolegomena? What would you add or subtract from the elements of a Christian philosophic prolegomena that I have discussed in this book?

2) Does Christianity have a metaphysic? How might the biblical method of knowing God by his deeds and words in history influence our understanding of God? What is the metaphysical substance of theism, Trinitarianism, and the doctrine of creation? How do people today use the word *metaphysics*? What is your metaphysic?

3) What does it mean to say that human beings are microcosms of macrocosms? What is society's attitude toward human nature? Biblically speaking, what is the difference in humanity and what moral difference does it make? What is the anthropological significance of the incarnation? What is Christian humanism? Are you a Christian humanist? Explain.

4) Why is epistemology so important? Describe our culture's current epistemic condition. What does natural and special revelation contribute to a Christian epistemology? What does narrative contribute, in particular the overarching biblical narrative? How are love, knowledge, and practice related? What do you know? How do you know it?

5) Why might ethics be the "end game" of philosophy (at least historically)? Do you think all people have a built-in sense of right and wrong? How does special revelation or the Bible contribute to moral philosophy? Explain the nature and importance of the vice and virtues traditions. Discuss the issue of the greatest good—the *summum bonum*—from

biblical and nonbiblical perspectives. How might ethics entail both consequences and duties? What and who are the antinomians? Explain your
own moral vision.

6) What are the differences between aesthetics, philosophy of art, and art
criticism? Explain Plato's views of aesthetics. What is beauty? Must art be
beautiful? Sketch a biblical view of the arts. What are some biblical insights
on dance and film? How might art reduce anxiety? What does your room
say about you aesthetically?

7) Why might some Christian philosophers fail to acknowledge Jesus Christ
as the exemplar and Lord of their calling as philosophers? What should we
learn from the things that worried Plato about the impact of philosophy on
young philosophers? To whom have you hitched your philosophical wagon?
What metaphilosophies of philosophy have been influential in shaping the
philosophic vocation historically? How has Max Weber's modern rendi-
tion of the scholar's vocation proven influential? In what ways should the
basic elements of the Christian gospel shape our understanding and practice of the Christian philosophic vocation?

# GLOSSARY

**Absolute Pantheism.** The metaphysical and theological view that god is all and all is god; from the Greek *pan* for "all" or "everything" and the Greek *theos* for "god." It is held by both Eastern and Western thinkers, sometimes with certain variations.

**Aesthetics.** Philosophical subdiscipline devoted to investigation of beauty and the arts and the experiences human beings have when they encounter them.

**Antithesis.** The inevitable choice people face in all realms of life between obedience and disobedience to God, between wisdom and foolishness, between life and death, and between blessing and cursing.

**Augustinianism.** The system of theology and philosophy derived from Saint Augustine, emphasizing the restless heart fulfilled in God and a Christian faith seeking understanding.

**Autonomy.** The quest by humans to be free and independent of God, subject not to his laws (heteronomy) but to none other than one's own law(s); literally, "self-law."

**Axiology.** The philosophic study of value, especially the values associated with ethics and aesthetics.

**Beauty.** A combination of qualities such as proportion, order, harmony, and color that pleases the senses, sight and sound in particular; a debate ensues over whether beauty is subjective or objective in nature.

**Coherence/Coherentism.** As a theory of truth, it is the idea that a statement must fit consistently with other beliefs in one's belief system; as a test of truth, if a statement does not fit with other beliefs in one's belief system, it is false.

**Common Grace.** The blessings, gifts, talents, and abilities that God bestows on all people, regardless of their relationship to him.

**Consequentialism.** In moral philosophy, the view that something is right if it brings about the desired results.

**Deism.** The "clockwork" view of God as the creator of the world but as one who no longer intervenes in its affairs historically or humanly; deism is theism minus immanence.

**Dualism.** A word with many possible meanings and uses depending on context; normally, it refers to something divided into two parts, one good, one not as good, if not actually evil.

**Empiricism.** An epistemological view that asserts that human knowledge is derived exclusively from the senses and experience.

**Epistemology.** The philosophic subdiscipline concerned with the study of knowledge; what one knows and how one knows it.

***Fides Quaerens Intellectum.*** A noted Latin phrase that literally means "faith seeking understanding"; often associated with Saint Augustine's view of the relationship of faith and reason, of Christianity and philosophy.

**Foundationalism (Strong and Weak).** An epistemological view that affirms that the house of knowledge must rest upon and be logically derived from an appropriate foundation, as a house rests on a foundation.

**Grace Restores Nature.** A theological and Christian philosophic viewpoint in which it is held that God's grace in Christ's redemption renews and restores all things in nature and culture.

**Greatest Good.** An ethical element that specifies what is the very best for human beings; see also *Summum Bonum.*

**Handmaiden.** A word used to describe the traditional view of philosophy as the helper or assistant to theology.

*Homo Adorans.* A designation of human beings as the kinds of creatures who worship and adore.

*Homo Faber.* A designation of human beings as the kinds of creatures who make (or fabricate) things.

*Homo Sapien.* A designation of human beings as the kinds of creatures who think and seek wisdom.

**Idealism.** A metaphysical view of reality, focusing on the mind and the contents of mind in the form of ideas; matter comes from mind.

*Imago Dei.* Latin expression referring to human beings as God's image.

**Incarnation.** Theological word used to describe Christ as Son of God coming to human beings in the flesh as fully man. It conveys the idea that in Jesus we see the perfect and permanent union of humanity and deity without either of these natures being impaired (*Oxford Dictionary of the Christian Church*).

**Justified True Belief.** A debated definition of knowledge, entailing trust in a true and justified claim about life and the world. In Plato's dialogue the *Theaetetus*, a definition of knowledge as true belief with an account.

**Logical Positivism.** A twentieth-century philosophical movement that holds that meaningful statements must be either true by definition (a triangle is a three-sided figure) or scientifically verified (three cats are in the room). As a movement, it eliminated much of traditional theology, metaphysics, and ethics by sharply distinguishing between verifiable, scientific facts and personal values.

**Metanarrative.** A way of referring to the grand or master story that defines life and the cosmos; some postmodernists hold metanarratives in great suspicion as potentially violent.

**Metaphysics.** A philosophic subdiscipline concerned with the investigation of reality in both the natural and supernatural realms; the quest to discover the really real as opposed to mere appearance.

**Monism.** A metaphysical position in which all things may be reduced to and explained by one thing, like water in Thales's system of thought.

**Naturalism.** A view of reality espousing nature and nature alone as the "whole show" (C. S. Lewis).

**Nominalism.** The metaphysical view that general terms are not referencing objectively existing universals, but that universals, like dog or man, are simply names ascribed to entities sharing common traits.

**Nonconsequentialism.** The ethical view that rules and duties are right and to be performed, regardless of results.

**Objective/Objectivity.** The metaphysical view that asserts that what is real and true is completely independent of human desire and observation.

**One and the Many.** The metaphysical quest to discover the one universal thing that unites and explains the many things that exist concretely as particulars.

**Ontology.** The metaphysical study of being and the kinds of beings that exist (especially ranked in order from higher to lower or lower to higher—the great chain of being).

*Palingenesis.* Greek word transliterated into English meaning "born again," that is, "regeneration."

**Panentheism.** God is *in* all things; all things are *in* God (note the infix en/in); a variant of pantheism.

*Philosophia christiana.* Latin for "Christian philosophy."

*Philosophie christliche.* German for "Christian philosophy."

**Pluralism.** The metaphysical view that reality consists of at least three (or possibly more) things.

**Polytheism.** The belief in the existence of many gods and/or goddesses.

**Pragmatism.** As a theory of truth, pragmatism asserts that what works is true; as a test for truth, if a proposition works, it is true.

**Presuppositions.** Etymologically speaking, a presupposition refers to that which is posited underneath in advance (Gordon Spykman). Presuppositions are the rails upon which the train of thought runs, often hidden, and taken for granted.

**Prolegomena.** Literally, this word means "a word spoken beforehand" and is a preliminary exercise to the study of any subject matter or discussion; the purpose of a prolegomena is to clarify the fundamental assumptions, methods, principles, and relationships that guide inquiries or discussions, especially academic ones.

**Realism.** The metaphysical view that asserts that what is real actually exists independently of human desire or observation.

**Reason/Rationalism.** In epistemology, reason refers to the principles of sound thinking; as a source of truth, it asserts that knowledge is derived from human logic and thinking; if *all* knowledge is deemed to proceed from human reasoning, then it is called "rationalism."

**Scientism.** A view of science that makes it the sum total of the way of knowing the world. Science is the whole epistemological show, the complete royal road to knowledge.

**Situationism/Situationalist.** An ethical view that technically posits the way of love as the only legitimate alternative to legalism and complete lawlessness.

**Skepticism.** An epistemic view that challenges the human ability to know the world either in whole or in part.

**Social Imaginary.** A term somewhat synonymous with worldview, but perhaps deeper as a reference to ways people imagine their social existence with others and the normative notions and images that underlie social expectations; an expression made famous by the Canadian philosopher Charles Taylor.

**Special Revelation.** A technical reference to the whole of Scripture as God's infallible Word made known through inspiration of the human authors; it is an epistemological position that claims human beings must be told by God what is true.

**Structure and Direction.** A metaphysical distinction derived from theological considerations between the ontological or structural goodness of all creation and the possibility of using the ontological or structural goodness of all creation in moral and ethical or immoral or unethical ways.

**Subjective/Subjectivity.** The metaphysical view that asserts that what is real depends entirely on human desire and observation.

*Summum Bonum.* Latin rendering for the expression the "greatest good"; as a moral or ethical concept, it conveys the aspiration to discover the best possible life for human persons.

**Teleology.** The metaphysical view that all things, great and small, have an aim, meaning, and purpose. It includes the philosophic search to discover that built-in aim, meaning, or purpose in all things, from human beings, to various objects, to the cosmos as a whole.

**Testimony.** The epistemological notion that states that most of what we know is conveyed to us by the words and messages of others, especially by authorities.

**Theism.** The standard view of God in the Western world, held by Jews, Muslims, Christians, and other theistic groups, that avers that God is all-powerful, all-knowing, all-present, immanent, and transcendent God of all things.

**Thomism.** The system of theology and philosophy derived from Saint Thomas Aquinas, emphasizing the fact that human understanding is perfected and completed by Christian faith.

**Trinitarianism.** The theistic view of God as consisting of one God in three separate, coequal, and coeternal persons—Father, Son, and Holy Spirit.

**Universals.** Refers metaphysically to permanent things, fixities, or ultimate presences that transcendentally exist and define concrete particular things that are in the world.

**Utilitarianism/Utilitarian.** An ethical view that emphasizes the greatest good for the greatest number.

*Weltanschauung.* German word for "worldview," coined by Immanuel Kant.

**Wisdom.** Often defined as "knowledge applied"; perhaps synonymous in Scripture with "knowledge that is always to be applied"; it denotes sound and serene judgments regarding the conduct of life (*Encyclopedia of Philosophy*).

**Worldview.** An embodied vision of the human heart about God, life, the world, and human beings; one's essential assumptions and interpretations about the meaning and purpose of all things.

Definitions of philosophical terms and names are readily available online:

Philosophy-Dictionary.org. http://www.philosophy-dictionary.org/.

Philosophy Pages. http://www.philosophypages.com/dy/index.htm.

# RESOURCES FOR FURTHER STUDY

Allen, Diogenes, and Eric O. Springsted. *Philosophy for Understanding Theology.* 2nd ed. Louisville: Westminster, 2007.

Audi, Robert, ed. *The Cambridge Dictionary of Philosophy.* 2nd ed. Cambridge, UK: Cambridge University Press, 1999.

Chervin, Ronda, and Eugene Kevane. *Love of Wisdom: An Introduction to Christian Philosophy.* San Francisco: Ignatius Press, 1988.

Clark, Kelly James, ed. *Philosophers Who Believe: The Spiritual Journeys of 11 Leading Thinkers.* Downers Grove, IL: InterVarsity, 1993.

Clark, Kelly James, Richard Lints, and James K. A. Smith. *101 Key Terms in Philosophy and Their Importance for Theology.* Louisville: Westminster, 2004.

Cowan, Steven B., and James S. Spiegel. *The Love of Wisdom: A Christian Introduction to Philosophy.* Nashville: B&H Academic, 2009.

DeWeese, Garrett J. *Doing Philosophy as a Christian.* Christian Worldview Integration Series. Downers Grove, IL: InterVarsity, 2011.

Evans, C. Stephen. *Pocket Dictionary of Apologetics and Philosophy of Religion: 300 Terms and Thinkers Clearly and Concisely Defined.* Downers Grove, IL: InterVarsity, 2002.

Geisler, Norman L., and Paul D. Feinberg, *Introduction to Philosophy: A Christian Perspective.* Grand Rapids, MI: Baker, 1980.

Grenz, Stanley J., and Jay T. Smith. *Pocket Dictionary of Ethics: Over 300 Terms and Ideas Clearly and Concisely Defined.* Downers Grove, IL: InterVarsity, 2003.

Kreeft, Peter. *The Philosophy of Jesus.* South Bend, IN: St. Augustine's Press, 2007.

Maritain, Jacques. *An Introduction to Philosophy.* 1930. Reprint, New York: Continuum, 2005.

Martin, Robert M. *The Philosopher's Dictionary.* 3rd ed. Peterborough, Ontario: Broadview Press, 2002.

McInerny, Ralph. *A Student's Guide to Philosophy.* Wilmington, DE: ISI Books, 1999.

Morris, Thomas V., ed. *God and the Philosophers: The Reconciliation of Faith and Reason.* New York: Oxford University Press, 1994.

Moser, Paul K., ed. *Jesus and Philosophy: New Essays.* New York: Cambridge University Press, 2009.

Pieper, Josef. *In Defense of Philosophy: The Power of the Mind for Good or Evil Consists in Argumentation.* Translated by Lothar Krauth. San Francisco: Ignatius Press, 1992.

Solomon, Robert K., and Kathleen M. Higgins. *The Big Questions: A Short Introduction to Philosophy.* 8th ed. Belmont, CA: Wadsworth, 2010.

# INDEX

# ✚ CHECK OUT THE OTHER BOOKS IN THE **RECLAIMING THE CHRISTIAN INTELLECTUAL TRADITION SERIES**

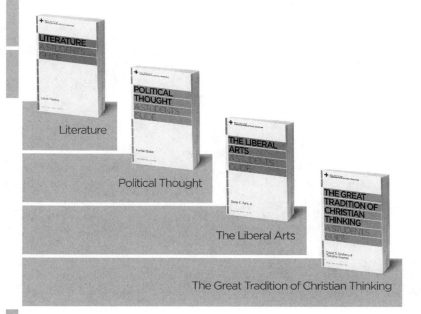

Literature

Political Thought

The Liberal Arts

The Great Tradition of Christian Thinking